Cambridge English Readers

Level 5

Series edi

Jungle Love

Margaret Johnson

CAMBRIDGE
UNIVERSITY PRESS

CAMBRIDGE
UNIVERSITY PRESS

University Printing House, Cambridge CB2 8BS, United Kingdom

One Liberty Plaza, 20th Floor, New York, NY 10006, USA

477 Williamstown Road, Port Melbourne, VIC 3207, Australia

314–321, 3rd Floor, Plot 3, Splendor Forum, Jasola District Centre, New Delhi – 110025, India

79 Anson Road, #06–04/06, Singapore 079906

Cambridge University Press is part of the University of Cambridge.

It furthers the University's mission by disseminating knowledge in the pursuit of education, learning and research at the highest international levels of excellence.

www.cambridge.org
Information on this title: www.cambridge.org/9780521750844

© Cambridge University Press 2002

First published 2002
Reprinted 2018

Printed in the United Kingdom by Hobbs the Printers Ltd

A catalogue record for this publication is available from the British Library

ISBN 978-0-521-75084-4 Paperback

Contents

Characters

Jennifer Wilson: a young woman on holiday in Belize
Lisa Casey: the young woman sharing Jennifer's room
Ian: another member of the holiday group
Caroline: Ian's girlfriend
Pete Dobson: engaged to Jennifer
Mary: the Belizean tour leader
Gary: a man in Jennifer's life in England
Aunt Rose: Mary's aunt
Ocean: a Belizean man
Frank: Lisa's brother
Sam: a Belizean guide

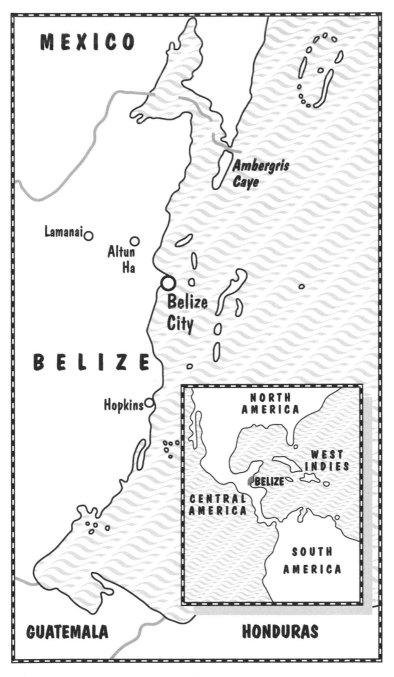

MEXICO

Ambergris
Caye

Lamanai

Altun
Ha

Belize
City

BELIZE

Hopkins

NORTH
AMERICA

WEST
INDIES

BELIZE

CENTRAL
AMERICA

SOUTH
AMERICA

GUATEMALA

HONDURAS

Chapter 1 *In the jungle*

Jennifer

At eleven o'clock this morning, I was standing at the edge of a rain forest with my eyes closed. The smell of the warm, wet leaves was so strong it was quite delicious and the sounds were magical; hundreds of different birds were singing unfamiliar songs in the treetops all around me. Somewhere, out in the heart of the jungle, wild animals were hunting for food. Belize is so mysterious and exciting – a place where anything could happen. And I, Jennifer Wilson, am here, a part of it all.

Unfortunately, so is Lisa. There we were today in this magical place and Lisa started her usual complaining.

'How could I be so stupid as to pick a tour with only one other single person on it?'

'What?' I turned unwillingly to look at her, not wanting to lose the magic of the ancient forest.

Lisa was looking at me moodily. 'Of all the tours in all the holiday brochures in all the world, I had to pick this one,' she complained. 'Six happy couples and you and me. It isn't fair; you should be a man.'

I had heard this statement at least three times before, so I closed my eyes to see if the magic would return. 'I'm sorry I'm such a disappointment to you.'

I heard Lisa sigh heavily. 'Oh, it isn't your fault, I suppose,' she said generously. 'I blame the holiday company. I mean, they should have arranged it better. Everybody knows a single person doesn't book onto a trip like this just to see the sights.'

I opened my eyes again, giving up on magic for a while.

'A single person on holiday alone is looking for a partner,' Lisa continued. 'It's obvious.'

'Well, I'm not,' I said, but Lisa didn't seem to believe me.

'Don't be silly,' she said. 'Of course you are.'

I knew there wasn't any point in trying to argue with her, so I shut up. Which is exactly what I wish Lisa would do from time to time. She loves talking, you see. About everything and everyone, but especially about herself. In the two weeks we've been travelling together, I've heard about: her family – her mum and a brother; her job – a manager in a London restaurant; and her flat – living room, kitchen, large bathroom and two bedrooms. I also know every tiny detail of every other holiday she's ever been on and about most of her ex-boyfriends. It's only too clear that Lisa *needs* to talk.

'Look,' I said, trying to escape, 'I'll see you later on, OK? I want to look for hummingbirds.'

But as usual Lisa didn't seem to want to be on her own. 'No, it's alright,' she said. 'I'll come with you. Although I don't understand why you're so interested in hummingbirds.'

'We don't get hummingbirds in England,' I reminded her.

'Well, you certainly do here in Central America!' she said. 'Thousands of them. Millions of them! There are six pages of them in Mary's bird book.' Mary's our tour leader, a girl of about our own age. She was born here in Belize and she's really nice.

'Speaking of Mary,' Lisa said, 'I think she's trying to get our attention. Hey, Mary! We're over here!' As Lisa shouted – very loudly – I watched every bird, including all the hummingbirds, fly away into the forest.

'You girls are going to miss what Sam has to tell you about the Mayan people!' Mary shouted back.

'Looks as if your hummingbirds will have to wait,' Lisa said.

I looked at her, doing my best to keep my feelings from my face. 'They've gone now anyway,' I pointed out.

'Oh well,' said Lisa with a little laugh, 'that's all right then, isn't it?'

*   *   *

'The ancient Mayans believed that everything in the jungle had power,' Sam, the guide, told us when we were all gathered together. 'Every animal, every tree, even the smallest insects on the ground, everything had power. They were all gods. And these gods could choose whether to be kind or angry to the people of the forest. Of course the Mayans wanted the gods to be kind to them so they gave them gifts to make them happy.'

'What sort of gifts?' someone asked.

'They gave the gods the gift of their lives,' Sam said, looking round at us all. 'Thousands of people have died right here to keep the gods happy.'

'How horrible!' someone else said.

I thought it was horrible too, but I also thought it was really interesting. I work as an illustrator, painting pictures for children's books, and as I listened to what Sam was telling us, I was almost painting pictures in my mind.

'To the Mayan Indians, it was an honour to be chosen for this sacrifice,' Sam continued. 'They did not fear it, as you or I would do. And sometimes they did not need to die. Sometimes the people were only asked to wound themselves to provide blood for the gods. Even the kings did this. Imagine it ladies and gentlemen; imagine thousands of people standing here where you are standing now, as the king climbed to the very top of this hill. Everyone watched the king as he slowly took a knife from his pocket,' Sam continued, using his hands to demonstrate the actions he was describing, 'a knife made from the spine or backbone of a fish, the stingray. This bone was sharp, ladies and gentlemen; very, very sharp. The king held the knife high above his head, and then he opened his clothes and quickly brought it down to make a wound in his body.'

'Was it always a king?' Lisa wanted to know now. 'Or were there queens in the days of the Mayans?'

'Yes,' Sam told her, 'sometimes there were queens, and yes, sometimes they had to make a sacrifice of their blood. They did this by using the spine of the stingray to make a wound in their tongue.'

'Oh no! How awful!' Lisa said, and, watching her, I couldn't help smiling.

Ian, one of the men in our group, was smiling too. 'No, Lisa,' he said, 'that wouldn't suit you at all, would it?'

Then Mary started to laugh. 'You're right, Ian. Lisa wouldn't be able to talk all the time!'

And suddenly everyone was laughing at Lisa.

9

'You're all horrible!' she complained, but I knew Lisa didn't mind. In fact, she was delighted. She was exactly where she loved to be most, at the centre of everyone's attention.

Sam began to speak again, telling us about an ancient game of football the Mayans had played; a bloody way of making peace between fighting villages, where the winners were killed as sacrifices to the gods, and suddenly I felt I'd had enough of blood and death. *And* Lisa's childish play-acting. Deciding to go and see if the hummingbirds had returned, I walked quietly away from the group and headed back towards the edge of the forest.

As I stood there under the trees, Sam's voice was a soft sound in the distance and I closed my eyes to listen to the birds. I was listening so hard that it came as quite a shock when there was a sudden noise behind me.

My heart started beating fast. 'Who's there?' I asked, opening my eyes and half expecting to see some wild cat or other dangerous animal.

But it was a man, not a wild cat. It was Ian.

'Sorry,' he said, standing there looking at me. 'Did I scare you? It's all right; I haven't got a stingray spine with me!'

I smiled, my heart slowing down again. 'I think Sam's stories have made me feel a bit nervous,' I said.

Ian grinned. 'I'm not surprised. He's talking about people's heads being cut off now. Horrible! I'm not very good with blood.'

'It's all very interesting, but I'm more keen on nature than history,' I said. 'Birds and animals. All these wonderful trees and flowers.'

'Yes, they're fantastic, aren't they?' he agreed, standing next to me and moving his head back to look right up into the top of a tall, very green tree.

While he was busy looking at the tree, I looked at him. I've recently illustrated a children's book about pirates; those robbers who once sailed their ships on the oceans and attacked other ships to steal their gold. I thought that if Ian were dressed in different clothes and wearing gold ear-rings, he would look like a pirate. It was easy to imagine him on his ship, a pirate captain with the wind blowing through his black hair.

He looked down and caught me staring at him.

'Is . . . is your wife interested in history?' I asked quickly, feeling embarrassed.

He gave a heavy sigh. 'Oh, Caroline,' he said. 'Yes. She's *extremely* interested in history.' He was about to say more when suddenly there was a loud scream from the top of a tree nearby.

With my mind still full of pirates and adventure, I was a bit scared at first. 'Goodness!' I said. 'What was that?'

'My guess is a monkey,' Ian said. 'A howler monkey. Let's go and see if I'm right.'

I followed him as he started to walk further into the forest. By now the noise was very loud indeed.

'Look! There they are.' Ian reached for my arm, turning me to face in the right direction. 'There's a pair of them, I think. Can you see?'

I looked up into the tree he was pointing at and saw two surprisingly small monkeys. 'Are they really making all that noise?' I asked, amazed. 'That's incredible.'

'Yes, isn't it?' Ian smiled, and I suddenly realised how

close he was standing to me. He seemed to realise it too, because he stopped laughing and looked down into my eyes.

'By the way,' he said, as the howler monkeys continued to scream above us, 'she isn't.'

'Sorry?' I said. 'Who isn't what?'

'Caroline,' he said. 'She isn't my wife.'

Chapter 2   *Zips*

Lisa

Day thirteen of the holiday and so far I've seen seven different hotel rooms, nine hundred and sixty-eight hummingbirds and the latest in a very long line of Mayan ruins – this time at Altun Ha or somewhere. By the time we got back to the hotel, I was hot, tired and desperate for a shower. The tour bus is unbelievably basic; forget air conditioning, half the windows don't even open properly. I'm not sure what we've paid our money *for*, to be honest. And today's trip *certainly* wasn't worth getting cooked for. All that stuff about sacrifices; Sam was obviously doing his best to shock us. Anyway, I've heard it all before on other holidays. *Better* holidays – to Africa, India and Mexico.

The difference being that in Africa there was Mark, the tall, dark engineer from Scotland, and in India there was Nigel, the red-haired footballer from Surrey. Whereas in Mexico . . . well, in Mexico there was Sven. Mmm, Sven. Now *he* was wonderful. All that blond hair and those blue, blue eyes. You see, if there was an interesting, sexy man in the group, I wouldn't mind how often I had to listen to boring tour guides talking about people being sacrificed.

Unfortunately, the only attractive man on this holiday is Ian, and Ian's going out with Caroline. However, they were definitely having an argument about something in the bus on the way back to the hotel. *And* Ian wandered off somewhere on his own at Altun Ha. Caroline looked very annoyed about it actually; she obviously had no idea where he'd got to.

Anyway, Caroline's going home in the morning. This holiday is either for two weeks or three weeks. Most people are staying for the full three weeks, but a few are leaving early, including Caroline, foolish woman. Imagine being so stupid as to leave an attractive man like Ian here all on his own. Doesn't she know the jungle is full of hungry hunters?

Smiling to myself, I finished my shower, then wound one of the hotel towels around myself and went into the bedroom to dress. Jennifer was still sitting on her bed reading a book.

Jennifer's *always* reading. If it isn't a book about the flowers or birds of Belize, then it's a historical novel or something. It's a complete waste of time trying to have a conversation with Jennifer when she's reading, but somehow I can't help trying. Well, it annoys her, you see, and annoying Jennifer is a great sport. Anyway, I think Jennifer *ought* to speak to me. We have been sharing hotel rooms for two weeks, after all.

'God!' I said to Jennifer's bent head, starting to dry myself with the towel. 'It's so hot in here. That cold shower hasn't made me feel any cooler.'

Jennifer didn't look up. 'No?' she said.

'I'm going to complain to Mary,' I continued, drying my back.

'Yes,' Jennifer said.

I sighed. 'What are you reading today?'

Jennifer finally looked up. 'Sorry?' she said, proving to me what I'd already guessed: she hadn't been listening.

'I asked what you were reading,' I said coldly, and Jennifer lifted her shoulders.

'Oh, it's a book by Thomas Hardy,' she said. *'Far From the Madding Crowd.'*

A book about getting away from people. How perfect for Jennifer. 'It doesn't sound like very much fun to me,' I told her.

'It's a wonderful book actually,' Jennifer said. 'The descriptions of the countryside are so realistic, I feel as if I'm actually there.'

She began to read again and I sighed. Why on earth would anyone want to pay out a huge amount of money to travel all the way here to Belize from England only to read a book about England when they got here? It makes no sense to me at all, it really doesn't. But then nothing much about Jennifer makes sense to me. We seem to be complete opposites.

I turned my back on Jennifer and reached for my suitcase to find something to wear for the evening. Because we're only staying at Ambergris Caye for one more night, I haven't bothered to unpack all my clothes. Most of them are still lying neatly in their plastic wallets. I always pack my clothes in plastic wallets; they've got zips at the top, so there's no chance of anything getting wet if it rains. And I can always find what I want quickly, because I've got one wallet for underwear, another wallet for socks and so on.

However, it does mean that I do have to undo a lot of zips to get out all the items of clothing I need. For example, to find the underwear, trousers, T-shirt and socks I needed now, I would have to unzip four plastic wallets altogether. And then, of course, they would all need to be zipped back up again.

I like the sound of the zips. It reminds me that the plastic wallets are a really practical idea. Not only that, but, although Jennifer's never said anything, I know the sound of the zips really annoys her. Her body goes all sort of stiff when I'm getting my clothes out of the wallets. She seems to hold her book tighter too.

'I soon get bored when I read,' I said, taking a T-shirt out of a wallet and zipping the wallet up again. *Zip*.

Jennifer looked at her book and didn't reply.

'I'm too active,' I tried again, opening another plastic wallet to take out my underwear. *Zip*.

Jennifer still didn't reply.

I reached for the plastic wallet containing a pair of jeans. *Zip*. I took the jeans out, then changed my mind. 'Oh no, I think I'll wear my other trousers,' I said, returning the jeans to their wallet. 'Jeans are too warm.' *Zip*.

By this time, Jennifer was finally looking at me.

'Are you admiring my plastic wallets?' I asked her sweetly.

'Well,' Jennifer said, her voice equally sweet, 'you certainly have a lot of them.'

'Yes,' I agreed, touching the plastic with pleasure. 'I thought of them after my holiday to Africa. It rained for a whole fortnight. Everyone's clothes were wet the whole time. It was amazing that none of us got really ill . . . '

Jennifer got off the bed.

'Where are you going?' I asked her.

'I think I'll go and read my book on the balcony,' she said. 'It might be cooler.'

'I doubt it,' I said. 'I think you'll find there's even less air conditioning outside.'

'Oh well.' Jennifer lifted her shoulders. 'I think I'll try it anyway. See you later.' And a second later she was gone.

'Well!' I said to myself, and then carried on getting dressed. There's no doubt about it, Jennifer really is one of the most unsociable girls I've ever met. *And* she's untidy. Her clothes are always left everywhere: on the chair, on her bed, even on the floor. Perhaps I ought to lend her some of my plastic wallets!

Sighing, I sat down in front of the mirror to brush my hair. This didn't take very long, because my hair's short. I always get it cut short before I go on holiday, otherwise the salt water makes it look like dried grass when I go swimming in the sea. Jennifer's hair is long – long and black and shiny. It's another reason I dislike her so much.

Jennifer might be boring, but she is pretty. And she leads an exciting life; or at least, she seems to, from the little she's told me. She lives in London anyway, which sounds exciting to me.

I don't live in London. I *want* to. I can't think of anything I'd like more than to live in London and have my own flat like Jennifer has. Maybe Jennifer reads books about people living in the English countryside but, believe me, she doesn't know anything about what life in the countryside is *really* like.

I do. In fact, I could write a book about it myself. I've lived in the countryside, Lower Tiveshell to be exact, all my life, and I can tell you it isn't the same as it's described in books at all. No, it's muddy, smelly and boring. And everyone always knows exactly what you're doing. Not that there's much *to* do. Anybody with any sense at all moves away to the nearest town as soon as they can – just as I would if it wasn't for Mum.

I haven't told Jennifer about that.

Actually, I haven't told Jennifer anything – or at least, I haven't told Jennifer the *truth* about anything. When I'm on holiday, I like to pretend my life is different from how it really is. Which was why I told Jennifer all those lies about a luxurious flat, a wonderful social life and a brilliant career as a restaurant manager.

Sadly, none of it's true. The truth is, I live with Mum in the house I was born in. Most of my friends moved away a long time ago, but Mum's old and her health isn't good, so she needs me to care for her. As for my job, although I *am* a restaurant manager, it's only in the local pub, the Black Bull. And the Black Bull is very different to the restaurant of my dreams. *Very* different.

All year long I have to cook fast food: pizzas and burgers and chips. Sometimes I feel as though I'll *never* get away. So that's why all year long I look forward to my holiday – it's what helps me to keep going. And usually I have such a fantastic time that, for three weeks, I really feel like the Lisa Casey I'm pretending to be.

Only so far this holiday hasn't turned out like that at all – and it isn't fair. However, all that is going to change very soon. I've got a plan!

Chapter 3 *Arguments and sunsets*

Jennifer

Lisa and her zips! I can't imagine how long it must have taken her to pack her suitcase with all those terrifyingly practical plastic wallets . . . days probably. Whereas I just threw everything into my case at the very last minute. I suppose that's why half of my clothes don't match and all of them are untidy. But at least I feel reasonably relaxed. Lisa never seems to be relaxed. It's exhausting just listening to her.

After I'd made my escape from her this afternoon, I settled down in a chair on the hotel balcony. People were walking past, but their voices were just a pleasant background sound.

I opened my book again and had just started to read when suddenly, I heard raised voices coming from the hotel room behind me. Whoever it was definitely sounded as if they were having an argument.

'Why do you need to take that much money with you?' I recognised Ian's voice immediately and realised that the room must be his – his and Caroline's. 'It leaves me with practically no cash at all,' he continued angrily, 'and you know the banks aren't open until Monday.'

Caroline said something back, but unfortunately she wasn't sitting close enough to the window for me to be able to hear her. But I could hear Ian very well indeed.

'Oh, take the money then!' he was shouting now. 'No, don't worry about me! I'm sure if I have a big enough dinner tonight, I can manage without eating anything again for two or three days!'

Next moment the door to their room opened and Ian hurried out, closing the door loudly behind him. When he saw me he paused, looking embarrassed. 'Oh,' he said. 'Sorry.' Then he hurried on. 'See you later. I need a beer. I think I can just about afford that at least!'

I watched him run down the wooden stairs at the side of the balcony and walk quickly away down the street. In the room behind me, Caroline was banging things about, obviously still angry. Then suddenly there was the sound of another door opening close by.

'Jennifer?' a voice called to me. 'Are you out there?'

Lisa! Again! Can't she leave me alone for more than five minutes? Jumping up quickly, I hurried down the wooden stairs to the street, just as Ian had done moments before.

'Jennifer?' As I ran down the dusty road, I could still hear Lisa calling after me, so I turned left down a side street to escape, only stopping when I reached the sea.

By then I was slightly out of breath, so I sat down on a bench and looked straight ahead at the view. Or at least my eyes were turned towards the pale sand and the blue sea, but I didn't really see them. I felt flat suddenly, as if some of the fun had gone out of the holiday. It wasn't just Lisa and needing to escape from her chatter and noise. It was . . . what? Caroline and Ian arguing? I wasn't entirely sure, but whatever it was, thoughts of home were suddenly with me, and thoughts of home are depressing.

Suddenly a face filled my mind. A pleasant, kindly face,

handsome really; Pete, my fiancé, the man I'm supposed to marry. I really didn't want to think about him, but somehow I couldn't help it. Perhaps it was because I'd been reading *Far From the Madding Crowd*. As I told Lisa, the book really brings the English countryside to life, and Pete loves the countryside. He loves it so much that he wants us to live in an old house in the countryside after we're married.

'Hey, pretty lady,' a very different voice to Pete's spoke to me suddenly, 'you want to go swimming with me tonight?'

Surprised out of my thoughts, I looked up to find a man grinning down at me. He was obviously a local man, not a tourist, and his smooth, dark skin looked very attractive in the last sunshine of the day.

I smiled back at him. 'I don't think so, thanks.'

'It's going to be a good moon tonight,' he continued, still smiling, trying to persuade me.

I picked up my book and stood up, determined not to let his smile affect me. 'I'm sure it is,' I said, keeping my voice friendly but trying my best to make it sound firm. 'But I'm going to watch it from the bar with a glass of rum.'

But the man didn't seem put off. In fact, his smile widened. 'Have to admit that sounds pretty good,' he said. 'But swimming in the moonlight with Ocean is even better. That's my name, Ocean.'

Ocean; it suited him.

'Yes,' he said, 'that moon, she turns the sea into magic water. You swim in magic water and your dreams they all come true.'

Ocean's voice was soft and deep, and his brown eyes looked straight into mine. He was an extremely attractive man. Too attractive.

I began to walk towards a jetty that stretched out into the sea. This old wooden walkway had a bar near the end of it. Fido's Bar. It was a perfect place to watch the sunset.

'Goodnight, Ocean,' I called, stepping from the silver sand onto the wooden jetty.

'Goodnight, pretty lady,' he said. 'I'm going to ask you about a moonlight swim again another time.'

I looked back and waved, knowing that if he invited me again, then next time I just might be persuaded to say yes.

Exactly as I'd decided to say yes when Gary from the sports centre had asked me to have dinner with him that time Pete was away on business.

You see, I'm afraid that basically I've got a slightly weak character. Sometimes I say yes when I know I should say no.

I'm not always a good girl.

Chapter 4   *Sunset at Fido's Bar*

Jennifer

The first person I saw when I entered Fido's Bar was Ian. He was looking miserable, sitting alone at a table for two with an almost empty glass in front of him.

I stood in the doorway, wondering whether I should leave quickly or go and join him, but then he looked up, making the decision for me.

'Jennifer,' he said. 'Hi. I'd offer to buy you a drink, but as you probably heard back at the hotel, I haven't got much money.'

'That's OK,' I said. 'Let me buy you one.'

'Oh, you don't have to do that,' he said.

I smiled, reaching for some money from my pocket. 'I know I don't,' I said 'but I'd like to. What are you drinking? Belikan beer?'

Belikan is the local beer made in Belize. When you don't fancy drinking rum, it's a delicious alternative.

'Yes, thanks,' he said.

I went over to the bar to order the drinks, and as I waited to be served, I noticed two women looking at Ian and whispering to each other about him. Clearly they found him attractive. So do I, I can't deny it. A woman would have to be very unusual not to find Ian attractive. However, I *don't* intend to do anything about it. *Not under any circumstances.* Ian's going out with Caroline and my life is already quite complicated enough with Pete and Gary.

He smiled at me as I carried the drinks back to the table. 'You've saved my life,' he told me. 'Come on, let's go outside.'

So I followed him outside, and we walked to the very end of the jetty where there was just a single table and two chairs.

'It's a bit like being on a boat,' I said as I sat down and drank some of my rum. The sea was on three sides of us, and I could see the sea grass moving about in the waves.

To be honest, I felt a bit nervous, being alone with Ian in such romantic surroundings. The table was obviously designed for a couple to watch the sunset together, not for two people who are definitely not going to be anything more than just friends.

'A few more drinks and it will probably *feel* like being on a boat too.' Ian was laughing, and I smiled and looked up at the sky.

It was changing colour quickly now, from orange to red and pink, and I thought, as I had several times since arriving in Belize, about how quickly the sun sets here.

'It's beautiful, isn't it?' I said to Ian, and he nodded.

'Yes,' he said, 'it really is.' He looked at me. 'I heard Mary saying you were an artist. Did you bring your paints with you?'

I shook my head. 'No,' I said. 'I never seem to want to paint when I'm on holiday.'

'What are your paintings like?' Ian wanted to know.

I thought about it. 'Well, it depends what I'm painting,' I told him, 'but usually they're quite small and very detailed. A bit old-fashioned, I suppose.'

'They sound nice,' he said.

I lifted my shoulders. 'They're right for me. I could never paint a big modern painting. It would be as wrong for me as being . . . an accountant or something.'

Ian smiled a little. 'Oh yes,' he joked. 'Accountants are *terrible* people.'

'Oh dear,' I said, feeling my face begin to turn almost as pink as the sky. 'You're an accountant, aren't you?'

'Yes, I'm afraid I am.' He smiled.

'Well, that's great!' I said quickly. 'I mean, I haven't got anything against accountants, it's just that I'm so hopeless at maths myself.'

'It's OK, Jennifer,' Ian said. 'I realise it's a boring job, but it does pay quite well. And somebody has to do it. The world needs accountants!'

'Yes,' I agreed, 'I certainly need mine.' I thought about my accountant, Roger. Comparing him with Ian, I had to smile. Although he's very dependable and probably saves me a lot of money, he's nothing like Ian at all. Roger's short, fat and bald, and doesn't speak a lot. Whereas, Ian, well . . . apart from being good to look at, Ian is very easy to talk to.

'I like a simple life,' he was saying. 'Good company, good food, a nice home and time to enjoy it. I'm not the type of person who's desperate for success. That drives Caroline crazy sometimes. Success is very important to her.' He drank some more of his beer, looking thoughtful. 'On the other hand, 'he said, almost speaking to himself, 'I expect there's lots about me that drives Caroline crazy.' He looked up at me, consciously putting a smile back on his face. 'Which reminds me, I'd better get back I suppose. It *is* her last night and there's supposed to be a goodbye dinner for everyone who's leaving tomorrow.

I'd forgotten about that. Actually, I didn't feel very enthusiastic about it. I quite like the other people on the tour, but I'm not used to being with people all the time, especially not people like Lisa who take so much of your energy.

'Do you think Caroline would mind if I missed her goodbye dinner?' I asked Ian. 'I think I'd like to stay here for a while and then go back and get an early night.'

'I expect you'll be forgiven,' he said, finishing his beer and getting up. 'I only wish I could stay with you. Anyway, enjoy your peace and quiet. I'll see you tomorrow. Oh, and thanks for the drink.' He gave me a final smile and began to move away.

'Bye,' I said, then sat back to watch him walk down the jetty. Ian walks like one of the jungle cats Mary told us about when she was speaking about the wild animals of Belize: a jaguar. I thought he was probably every bit as dangerous as a jaguar too. It surely wasn't very nice of him to say some of those things about Caroline to me. I wouldn't like it if he were my boyfriend.

Not that he's ever going to be my boyfriend. Men are too much trouble altogether. If they're not smiling into your eyes behind their girlfriend's back like Ian, then they're doing their best to make you live in some falling down old cottage miles from anywhere; the way Pete's trying to with me.

Or else they're threatening you.

Just like Gary after our night out together. He calmly told me that he knew Pete, and that if I didn't agree to see him again, he'd tell Pete we'd spent the night together. There's a word to describe that sort of behaviour; that word is *blackmail*.

Just as I was finishing my drink, I heard footsteps approaching along the jetty and looked up, wondering if it was Ian returning. But it wasn't Ian at all, it was Ocean. And he was still smiling at me.

'Now, pretty lady,' he said, sitting himself down in Ian's empty chair, 'I just *know* a swim in the magic moonlight is a good idea for you. I want you to say yes.'

The final light of the sun was shining on his dark skin, turning it a beautiful reddish-brown. It was very easy to believe in magic as I looked into his eyes. And suddenly I was smiling.

'All right,' I heard myself saying. 'Let's go.'

Chapter 5   *A breakfast message*

Lisa

Today's day fourteen of the holiday and, for once, I was in a really good mood at breakfast. Jennifer was still asleep, which meant a breakfast with no boring conversations about hummingbirds, Mayan ruins or historical novels. But better than that, Caroline has gone! While I was drinking coffee and eating fruit in the hotel dining room, she was at Belize City airport waiting for her flight to Houston!

This means, of course, that Ian is all on his own; but not for long! I don't feel at all guilty about my plans to break up Ian and Caroline because Caroline's so boring. Even more boring than Jennifer, if that's possible. All she talks about is her work. That's why she's going back early, to go back to work. Caroline is dull, dull, dull, and Ian is far too good for her. What he needs is someone like me. No, not someone *like* me – *me*. He needs me, and that's just what he's going to get.

Just as I was finishing my breakfast, Mary came into the dining room and sat down at my table. 'Morning, Lisa,' she said. 'You're looking very pleased with yourself. In fact, you look a lot like you're up to no good.'

I made my face as innocent as I could. 'Who, me?' I asked, raising my eyebrows.

'Yes,' Mary said, pointing a finger at me across the table.

'You, Lisa Casey. Trouble is your middle name, and don't you go denying it. I've met plenty of people like you before now. Where's your friend this morning, anyway?'

I knew she must be talking about Jennifer, but since Jennifer most definitely *isn't* my friend, I pretended not to understand. 'Friend?' I said. 'What friend's that?'

Mary frowned at me. 'Your roommate, the person you share a room with, Jennifer. I haven't seen her yet today and I've got an urgent message for her.'

'The last time I saw Jennifer she was still asleep in her bed,' I said.

'Still asleep?' Mary said crossly. 'Doesn't she know we have a boat to catch in half an hour?'

I couldn't help smiling at the thought of Jennifer being in trouble. 'I guess she doesn't know,' I said. 'Either that or she doesn't care. She didn't even bother to join us for dinner last night. I don't know where she went, but it was really late when she got back to the hotel. She woke me up.' I leaned forward towards Mary across the table. 'Actually, I think she might have been a bit . . . you know, *drunk*.'

Mary said a few local words I couldn't understand, but which I guessed were swear words, then pushed her chair back. 'Well, will you wake her up for me please?' she asked. 'I've got to pay our hotel bill. And tell her not to be late!'

'All right,' I agreed.

'Thanks,' said Mary. She began to walk away, then turned back. 'Oh, and can *you* give her this message?'

Mary offered me an envelope, but when I reached out to take it from her, she didn't let go of it straightaway.

'Don't go reading it now, will you, Lisa?' Mary warned me. 'That's a private message for Jennifer, OK?'

'What do you take me for, Mary?' I said, pretending she'd hurt my feelings – because, of course, I *had* been intending to read Jennifer's message as soon as Mary had gone. 'Of course I won't read it!'

I could see that she didn't really believe me. 'Well, see that you don't,' she said, letting go of the envelope and pointing a finger at me again. 'I'm going to ask Jennifer later on if that envelope was opened.'

'Mary,' I told her, 'I think you should have been a schoolteacher rather than a tour leader.'

Mary laughed at that. 'Girl,' she said, 'there's not much difference between the two jobs! Not when I've got people like you on the tour!' She gave me a cheerful wave and went out to reception to pay the bill.

I like Mary. It doesn't bother me at all that she seems to have such a bad opinion of me. Mary understands me. It was only a pity that this meant I couldn't open the envelope to read Jennifer's message, but I made up my mind to find some other way of discovering what it said.

I was just about to get up and go to our room to wake Jennifer, when Jennifer herself appeared in the entrance to the dining room. Her face was very pale and she was wearing sunglasses, even though she was indoors. It was only too obvious she'd had a late night.

'Morning,' she said to me faintly, sitting down carefully in the chair Mary had just left.

'Hi,' I said, and immediately Jennifer pulled a face.

'Would you mind speaking a bit more quietly?' she asked. 'I've got a headache.'

'I thought you might have,' I said. 'Where did you get to last night anyway?'

Jennifer poured herself a glass of orange juice with a slightly shaking hand. 'Oh,' she said, 'here and there. I had a few drinks and then I went for a swim.'

'In the dark?' I asked, puzzled, and then Jennifer smiled what I can only call a satisfied little smile and drank some of her orange juice, looking at me across the table through her sunglasses.

'There was a wonderful moon last night, actually,' she said, and something about the little smile and the satisfied sound of her voice almost made me want to hit her. I honestly can't remember when anybody last annoyed me so much. That woman is going to drive me completely crazy before long. If it hadn't been for the message, I'd have left her to eat her breakfast all on her own, but actually, I was very curious to find out what was so urgent.

'This is for you,' I said, throwing the envelope in her direction and narrowly missing her glass of orange juice. 'Mary's just given it to me.'

Jennifer looked at the envelope, her smile instantly disappearing. Then she picked up her glass again and drank some more of the juice.

I looked at her, tapping my fingers on the table impatiently. 'Well,' I said, 'aren't you going to see what it says?'

Very slowly Jennifer put down her glass, picked up the envelope and opened it. Then she looked down inside the envelope, trying to read the message without removing the note. Only when this proved to be impossible did she finally take the piece of paper out. She read it quickly, replaced it in the envelope and picked up her orange juice once again, her face looking very pale.

I felt like screaming, I really did. 'Well?' I said. 'Who's it from?'

Jennifer looked at me calmly through her sunglasses. 'It's from my fiancé, Pete,' she said. 'He says if I don't phone him back in the next few hours, he's going to break off our engagement.'

Chapter 6 *Snake on the road*

Jennifer

I have to say that the message Lisa gave me from Pete at breakfast came as rather a shock. It certainly made my headache worse anyway, and somehow, in the rush to get ready to leave, I didn't manage to get to a phone. No, I suppose that isn't true. If I'd really wanted to phone Pete, then I would have phoned him. But what I actually did was finish my orange juice. Then I went back up to the room to finish packing, and took my case down to the jetty where our boat was waiting to leave for Hopkins, the next place on our trip. As I got into the boat and we set off, I sat and watched Fido's Bar getting smaller and smaller, knowing that by the time we arrived at Hopkins it would be too late.

'You haven't phoned him, have you?' Lisa asked, and I shook my head.

'No,' I said, 'I haven't.'

She was obviously desperate to know the whole story, but I just didn't feel like talking about it. Finally she got fed up and started speaking to Mary, leaving me with my thoughts.

They were dark thoughts. Pete's message could only mean one thing: Gary's decided to tell him about our night together. Well, I'm not entirely surprised. Gary was extremely angry when I refused to meet up with him again.

He accused me of 'using' him, and a whole lot more besides. The knowledge that this is probably true doesn't make me feel any better.

After the boat there was a bus ride which took us past brightly painted wooden houses and then along one of Belize's many reddish-brown dirt roads. As the bus went along, I tried to make myself concentrate on the village we were heading for. I've been really looking forward to the time in Hopkins. We're staying in basic huts with thatched roofs made from dried grass. The huts are situated right on the beach and belong to a group of local women, who cook delicious traditional food for their guests. It all sounds like great fun, but somehow Pete's message this morning took away all the excitement.

If I'm really honest, I'm quite glad to think that my engagement to Pete might be over. However, I also feel very guilty about feeling glad. I know I should never have agreed to marry him in the first place, but he asked me when several of my friends had just got engaged. I suppose I was probably feeling a bit lonely and left out of all the excitement, and I just got carried away. And I do *like* Pete; I like him a lot. I'm just not in *love* with him.

For a while I thought I was in love with him. It was very nice to have someone so keen on me, bringing me flowers and presents and arranging romantic treats for me all the time. At least it was nice at first. Then, bit by bit, the flowers and the gifts started to make me feel *crowded*.

That's probably why I agreed to go out with Gary, though I know that wasn't the only reason. I've got an unfortunate habit of letting things happen to me instead of deciding for myself what I want to do and, in the end, I'm the one who suffers. Like the time when I was still at school and my best friend Gina persuaded me it would be a good idea for us to hide in the art cupboard. We stood in there in the darkness, listening to the art lesson in the room next door and trying not to laugh. Except it soon got boring, because Mr Lomax, the art teacher, didn't even notice we weren't in class. We couldn't leave the cupboard because we would get into trouble, so we just had to wait until the lesson was over and everyone had gone. But then another class came into the room straightaway. We were in that cupboard for three hours altogether!

Gina was always getting me into trouble. Somehow I just couldn't say no to her suggestions. I let things just happen to me, and I still do really.

Even this holiday. OK, I decided I needed to go away as soon as possible and I wanted to have an adventurous kind of holiday, but I didn't sit down with a pile of travel books and make a logical decision. No, I just phoned the travel company, asked them what they'd got and chose Belize because someone had cancelled at the last minute. Until then I didn't know anything about the country at all; in fact, I'd hardly even *heard* of it. Fortunately I love Belize, so this was a happy accident.

But Pete's another story. First I let my engagement to him just happen, and then there was the Gary experience. It was very wrong of me and I feel really bad that I unintentionally hurt him.

Suddenly Mary's excited voice broke into my thoughts, and, to my surprise, I noticed the bus was stopping. Looking out, I could see nothing but forest; we appeared to be in the middle of nowhere.

'What's wrong, Mary?' someone asked.

'Nothing's wrong.' She smiled at us from the front of the bus. 'Just a little something exciting for the nature lovers in the group.' She pointed out of the front window of the bus. 'A snake.'

I looked and saw a huge brown snake crossing the road in front of us.

'Don't worry yourselves,' Mary continued. 'It isn't poisonous. If you want to take a closer look you can get out. Anyone who's scared can stay in the bus.'

I got out. I'm not particularly interested in snakes, but they don't bother me, and it was a good opportunity to stretch my legs. I took my binoculars with me to look for interesting birds. Actually it was nice to be doing something other than just thinking about Pete and what a horrible person I am.

Lifting the binoculars to my eyes, I pointed them towards the forest, swinging them round to search the branches. I was just trying to decide whether some bright red spots high up in a tree were flowers or a group of parrots, when I heard someone approaching me. Looking round, I saw it was Ian.

'Oh,' I said. 'Hello.'

Something about my voice made him pause. 'Oh. Would you rather be on your own. I'm not disturbing you, am I?' he asked, and I quickly smiled.

'No, of course not. I'm only on my own because Lisa stayed in the bus,' I said. 'She doesn't like snakes.'

Actually, that's typical of her. She's always going on about how she's travelled all over the world on holidays like this. Well, the countries she says she's visited are supposed to have the biggest, most poisonous snakes of all. You'd think she'd be used to them by now.

'Have you seen anything interesting?' Ian asked, and I saw he had his own binoculars with him.

I pointed to the tree I'd been looking at. 'I thought those might be parrots, but as they haven't moved, I think they must be flowers.'

Ian looked at the tree through his binoculars for a while, then smiled down at me. 'Yes, I think they're flowers,' he said. 'Either that, or dead parrots that haven't fallen out of the tree yet.'

I knew he was joking, but I pretended to take him seriously. 'I suppose they could be,' I said. 'And yet why would so many birds die at the same time?'

'Perhaps they were sacrificed to make the God of the Trees happy,' Ian said, and I laughed.

He put down his binoculars and looked at me. 'That's the first time I've heard you laugh all day,' he said. 'I've been watching you. You look really sad.'

I kicked the ground with my walking boot. 'Oh,' I said, pulling a face, 'I'm not really sad. I just don't feel very proud of myself today.'

'I see,' he said. 'Actually, I must admit I know what's happened. I overheard Lisa talking about it. I'm sorry.'

For a moment I felt angry with Lisa, but then I sighed. If I know Lisa, then everyone on the tour will soon know about my broken engagement, but after all, does it really matter if they do?

'If it helps you at all,' Ian was saying softly, 'you aren't the only one to find themselves suddenly single.'

I looked up at him quickly. 'You don't mean . . .?'

He nodded. 'Yes, I do, actually,' he said. 'As from this morning at the airport, Caroline and I are no longer a couple. It just wasn't working.' He stared deep into my eyes. 'We've broken up,' he said.

Chapter 7 *Fishing at Hopkins*

Lisa

Another eight uncomfortable hours bumping along on that antique tour bus. I really am going to complain about it. With the prices they charge, it just isn't good enough. They should give us some money back.

To be exact, I suppose there were only seven and a half hours of actual bumping along. Mary had the bright idea of stopping and looking at that snake, so I had to sit in the bus and watch Jennifer laughing with Ian at the side of the road for the other thirty minutes!

Still, as soon as we arrived here at Hopkins, she left her bag in our hut and disappeared somewhere, thank goodness, leaving me in peace to get busy with my make-up and hairbrush. With Caroline gone, I don't intend to waste any time, you see. Hunters have to move quickly to be sure of success!

Just as I was putting on some lipstick, Mary put her head round the door.

'Hey, Lisa,' she said, 'I'm looking for Jennifer again. Is she here?'

I looked up. 'No,' I said. 'I've no idea where she is and, I have to tell you, I don't care much.'

'Well,' said Mary, 'somebody cares. That man of hers, Pete. He phoned here with another message for her. He must be very keen on her to find out the telephone number of *this* place.' She laughed, then almost immediately frowned as she noticed my lipstick. 'Hey, why are you getting all dressed up? I hate to disappoint you, girl, but there's no nightclub at Hopkins. Not much of anything here except the sea and the sand.'

'Yes, I had noticed that,' I said, pressing a tissue onto my lips to remove any extra lipstick. 'Anyway, do you want me to give Jennifer a message when I see her?'

Mary thought about it. 'OK,' she said at last. 'I didn't write it down this time. Just tell her Pete says . . . now hold on a minute and let me get this right . . . oh yes, Pete says, he's sorry, it isn't too late, and she can have all the time to think that she likes. You got that?'

I repeated the message and Mary nodded. 'OK girl, thank you. See you at seven o'clock for dinner. And don't you go spoiling that lipstick by kissing any fishermen now, will you?'

With that, Mary left the hut. I gave a final look in the mirror and was about to follow her outside, when something made me turn back. Jennifer's bag was where she'd left it, on her bed, and, sticking out of the front pocket, was her address book. Almost before I knew I was going to do it, I'd reached out and taken the small black book from the pocket. Well, all's fair in love and war, isn't it? Quickly turning the pages, I found the names listed under the letter 'P'. There was a Paula, the number of a pizza delivery service and . . . Pete. There were two numbers listed for him, a home number and a work number. I took the book over to my own bag, found a pen and a piece of paper, and wrote both numbers down. Then

I carefully returned Jennifer's address book to her bag pocket and left the hut.

If I think Jennifer is going to be a threat in any way at all, then Pete's number might be useful. Especially after what Mary told me.

Outside, I stood on the sand for a while, looking around me. A gentle wind was blowing towards me from the water, and I was glad I'd decided to wear a long skirt with my bikini top. The soft material was blowing around my legs in a way I knew was attractive. All I needed to do now was find Ian.

But apart from the group of huts with their thatched roofs, there was nothing but the sand, the sea and the tall trees. Ian was nowhere to be seen. In fact, neither was anyone else. Either everyone had disappeared for a walk like Jennifer, or else they were having a sleep after the journey.

Then, just as I was beginning to feel depressed, I saw him. He was sitting on the sand a hundred metres or so away, looking at something out to sea through his binoculars. Taking a deep breath to help me to feel calm and in control, I ran a final hand over my hair and walked across the sand towards him. When he didn't look round at first, I gave a little cough and at last he turned, lowering his binoculars.

'Hi,' he said, and to my pleasure, I saw him notice my skirt and bikini top.

'What are you up to all alone?' I asked.

'Watching a pelican catching fish,' he told me. 'Look, there he goes again.'

I looked up, just in time to witness a lot of water shooting up into the sky where the large bird had gone into the sea. It was as if a bomb had exploded.

Ian laughed at my surprised expression. 'I know, they look funny, don't they?' he said. 'But appearances can fool you; pelicans might look as if they're going to sink like stones, but they're actually excellent at fishing – catch a fish every time.' He pointed at the pelican which was now coming back out of the water. Its wings were so big and so wet it almost looked as if it wouldn't manage to fly, but somehow it did.

'There you are, you see – he's got another one,' Ian said, as the pelican flew to a narrow wooden jetty to eat his catch.

I sat down beside Ian on the sand, carefully arranging my skirt as I did so. The sexy effect of the soft material would be quite lost if it suddenly blew right over my head. 'Do you like watching birds?' I asked him.

Ian was watching me arrange my skirt around my legs. 'Yes,' he said slowly, lifting his face to look straight into my eyes. 'I do.'

I stared back at him. 'I saw some fantastic birds when I was in Africa,' I told him softly, still running my hand over my legs through the soft cloth of my skirt.

'I'm quite sure you did,' he said, and smiled at me slowly before turning away and lifting his binoculars to his eyes.

'The flamingos were amazing,' I went on, hoping to get his attention back. 'There were thousands and thousands of them, on one lake. *Millions* of them. It was as if the whole lake was pink.'

'Lovely,' Ian said, watching the pelican through his binoculars.

'But they're such ridiculous birds, aren't they?' By now I was definitely feeling jealous of the pelican.

Ian still didn't lower his binoculars. 'Are they?' he asked.

'Yes,' I said. 'How they stand on one leg. Well, one flamingo looks a bit stupid but, I have to say, when millions of them are all standing there with those long necks, they're just . . .'

'Amazing?' Ian suggested, and there was something about his voice that made me feel suddenly foolish. He was laughing at me.

'Well, yes,' I said, then shut up. Somehow this conversation wasn't going the way I wanted it to at all, and now I couldn't think of anything else to say. If only he would put those binoculars down!

'I'm looking forward to trying the local food at dinner tonight,' I said a little desperately, and Ian laughed.

'Yes,' he said, 'I have noticed you seem to enjoy your meals.'

I frowned at that. 'What do you mean?' I asked him, feeling annoyed. It almost sounded as if Ian was accusing me of being greedy.

Finally he put down the binoculars and looked at me. 'Oh, don't get me wrong. There's nothing wrong with enjoying your food,' he said. 'Caroline's *always* worrying about how much fat she's eating and it's extremely boring.'

That immediately cheered me up. It definitely didn't sound as if he was happy with Caroline.

'Caroline's very independent, isn't she?' I said, drawing a picture in the sand with my finger.

Ian lifted his shoulders. 'Yes, I suppose she is,' he said, 'but I've never minded about that, actually. I find independent, successful women attractive.' The way he looked straight into my eyes as he said this seemed to give his words an extra meaning, a meaning intended especially for *me*. 'But,' he continued, 'it's also nice to be needed by someone a bit. And I think your partner should share your interests, or at least, some of them. Bird-watching, for example. Caroline can't stand bird-watching.'

'Oh, I'm very interested in bird-watching,' I lied, and he looked at me, surprised.

'Are you?' There was open doubt in Ian's voice, and I felt my face grow slightly pink.

'Yes,' I said quickly, 'I am.'

'That's good,' Ian nodded. 'Which birds are your favourites on this holiday so far?'

'Um . . .' I thought hard, but my mind felt horribly empty. 'The yellow ones,' I said at last, and Ian smiled.

'Yellow ones?'

'The er . . . biggish ones.'

'Golden orioles?' Ian suggested, and I nodded quickly.

'Yes, that's it,' I said. 'Orioles.' Then I decided to be honest. 'Actually,' I said, 'I don't really know very much about birds, but I'm very interested in finding out. Very interested.'

Ian looked at me for a while. 'Well,' he said at last, 'in that case, come over here and try the binoculars. Take a look at my pelican.'

'You'll need to show me what to do,' I said, sensing an opportunity to get closer to him. 'I'm no good with binoculars. By the time I've managed to point them in the right direction, whatever I want to look at has usually disappeared.'

He fell for it. 'Come on then,' he said, smiling. 'Come over here. I'll show you what to do.'

Which was how I ended up exactly where I intended to end up when I first started to walk across the sand towards Ian – in his arms. OK, so he wasn't holding me in his arms so that he could *kiss* me, he just had his arms around me to help me to get the binoculars in the right position. But it was a start!

Chapter 8   *Oranges and kisses*

Jennifer

When we arrived here at Hopkins, I decided to leave my unpacking until later and to go for a walk along the shore.

It's all so beautiful: the blue ocean with little brightly coloured fishing boats sailing on it, and the perfect white sand with tall palm trees moving about in the wind. For the first time I really wished I'd brought my painting equipment with me; the scene would make a lovely picture.

But as I didn't have my paints, I decided to look for seashells as I walked, making a collection of them in my sun-hat to take home.

After a little while, I found a jetty and, walking to the end of it, I sat down and let my legs hang over the edge, placing my sun-hat full of seashells beside me. A sudden noise made me jump, and, looking up, I saw a pelican rising from the sea with a fish in its bill. The fish was so heavy that the bird seemed to be having trouble flying, and I watched until I saw it settle safely on a neighbouring jetty to eat its catch.

In some ways, I wish I could stay here forever; find myself a little house and paint pictures of pelicans and parrots. Life would certainly be a lot less complicated.

But then no doubt I'd soon get bored of such a lifestyle. It would probably be *too* simple. And too perfect, if such a thing were possible. And if I think about it, it's much the same as the lifestyle Pete wants me to agree to. A nice little house, beautiful countryside, time to paint my pictures all day long . . . At least, that's the way *he* sees it. But that's never how it works out, is it? What time is there left for painting after you've done the housework, driven for miles to get the shopping and taken the children to school? And that would be the reality because Pete most definitely wants to be a father.

I want to be a mother one day, or at least I think I do. But I don't want to be rushed into it. I don't feel ready for all of that just yet.

No, all in all, it's just as well that Pete *has* found out about Gary. Oh, he'll be hurt for a while, but now he has a chance to meet someone who really cares about him. Someone who thinks that a marriage and babies and a home in the countryside are a dream come true.

As I sat there on the jetty, a little voice inside me asked, 'And you? What do *you* want?' And then I remembered another voice, a warm Caribbean voice, talking to me about moonlight and magic; Ocean. 'You swim in magic water and your dreams they all come true.' The trouble is, I don't know what my dreams are. So how can they come true?

I have no idea why, but pictures of Ian suddenly filled my mind: Ian smiling down at me in the forest when we'd seen the howler monkeys; Ian on the jetty outside Fido's Bar, his face coloured by the sunset; Ian joking with me earlier today about whether the tree was full of flowers or dead parrots.

I shook my head, not liking the way my thoughts were going. I'd only just become an ex-fiancée. Surely I wasn't starting to think about Ian in romantic terms?

'My, my,' said a voice behind me, 'you're frowning hard, girl!' It was Mary; I'd been so deep in thought I hadn't heard her walking up the jetty towards me.

'Oh hi, Mary,' I said, doing my best to smile at her. 'Sorry.'

She sat down beside me. 'Hey, don't worry about it!' she said cheerfully. 'Everybody feels down some of the time. But at least your man's still mad about you. That doesn't seem like such a big problem to me.'

'I think Pete's probably mad *with* me, not *about* me,' I said, and she frowned.

'That Lisa didn't give you the message, did she?' she said, sounding annoyed, and I shook my head.

'I haven't seen Lisa since we arrived here,' I told her.

Mary sighed. 'OK, I'll forgive her then, I suppose. This time. Anyway, your man phoned the office. I think you'd better phone him back, girl. Sounds like he doesn't want to break up with you any more.'

'Oh,' I said, and sighed so heavily that Mary looked at me.

'But *you* want to break up with *him*, right?'

She'd guessed correctly, and I nodded. 'Yes,' I said, 'I think I do.'

'OK,' Mary was saying, 'if you're sure that's what you want. He sounds like a nice man though, girl, and there aren't too many of those around.' Mary got to her feet and stood there looking down at me. 'But please, phone him back anyway. Be kind to me. I'm a tour leader, not a private secretary!'

I smiled. 'OK, Mary.'

She nodded. 'Good. The ladies here have got a phone in the office. Let's go back and arrange for you to use it.'

While we walked, Mary told me about her plans to give up being a tour leader to go to America to study at university – just as soon as she's saved enough money. I was interested, especially when she told me she wants to study marine biology in the States. Then, she intends to return to Belize to help save the animals living in the ocean around here. But I know I'd have been even more interested in Mary's plans if I hadn't been thinking about the phone call I had to make.

By the time we reached the office, my mouth was feeling really dry and I was very nervous. My hand was even shaking slightly as I dialled Pete's number.

I waited for a moment, listening to the telephone ring thousands of miles away, and then suddenly I heard Pete's voice.

'Pete . . . ?'

'You've reached Pete Dobson's phone. Sorry I can't take your call right now . . . '

Pete's answerphone! I listened to the rest of the message, but then I hung up without speaking. I couldn't leave a message to say I didn't want to marry him. It just wouldn't have been fair. I decided to try later.

'Dinner is ready, Miss,' one of the ladies told me, smiling cheerfully, and I smiled back as best I could and went into the big hut. There was a vacant seat next to Mary, so I sat down in it.

'OK?' she asked me, and I lifted my shoulders.

'He wasn't there,' I told her. 'I'll have to try later.' I felt guilty somehow, and I hadn't even managed to speak to Pete. How am I going to feel after I *have* spoken to him?

One of the ladies put a plate of food in front of me; it was the traditional Belizean dish of chicken, rice and beans. I've eaten it many times before on this holiday and it's tasty enough, although sometimes lately I've found myself wishing I could have a nice hot curry instead. But just then I didn't really feel like eating anything.

Ian was sitting at the other end of the long table, next to Lisa. As I looked in his direction, he caught my eye and raised his wine glass. I made a poor attempt at a smile and, as I did so, I noticed Lisa frowning. Next moment she touched Ian's arm to attract his attention and he turned away.

'That girl is doing some hunting,' Mary observed, and suddenly I realised she was right. Lisa's face was close to Ian's; she was whispering something into his ear and laughing.

I'm not sure why I felt surprised. Lisa's certainly made no secret of the fact that she wants to meet a man on this holiday.

'You all right, Jennifer?' Mary asked me. 'You're frowning again. Don't worry, you can make your telephone call tomorrow and then everything will be OK.'

I nodded but was glad when someone else spoke to Mary and she turned away. Mary always seems to know what I'm feeling. Even when I'm not sure what I'm feeling myself!

When dinner was over, I left everyone to it and went outside onto the beach. It was still beautiful, even though darkness had fallen. The palm trees were moving about in the gentle wind and in front of me the waves were rolling gently onto the shore. Everything was so incredibly peaceful, even with the sound of music and laughter coming from the big hut behind me, and I soon felt more at peace myself.

It would be good really if Ian and Lisa got together, I told myself. It might stop me getting straight into another relationship by accident. That's the last thing I need.

Taking off my shoes, I began to walk through the water at the edge of the shore. Just then the moon came out from behind a cloud, throwing silver light onto the waves. It was so lovely; almost as if there were jewels dancing on the water, and I stopped to look at it, thinking about all the special ways I would enjoy being on my own, once I properly ended my relationship with Pete: I could stay up all night painting pictures; stay in bed all day on Sundays; get dressed up and go out with my friends to nightclubs. Except, I reminded myself, most of my friends are married now. Oh well, I'll just have to make some new friends to go to night clubs with . . .

Suddenly there was a voice behind me. It made me almost jump out of my skin.

'Lovely, isn't it?'

Ian.

My heart gave a little jump of pleasure at seeing him – oh no! – and I looked around for Lisa, but she was nowhere to be seen. 'You surprised me!' I said, suddenly not feeling peaceful any longer.

'Sorry.' He smiled. 'I thought you'd heard me.'

I shook my head. 'No. I was concentrating on the view. Where's Lisa?'

'Inside playing some game with oranges,' he said.

'Oranges?'

'Mary's organised some party games. I decided to make my escape.'

I knew the game he was talking about. It involves passing an orange along a row of people without using your hands. Most people use their chin. It gets you very close to people. *Very* close. I could imagine Lisa being extremely keen to pass an orange to Ian.

I turned to face the water again, but somehow I couldn't see my new single life properly any longer; I was too conscious of Ian standing behind me.

'I thought you might like to try it,' I heard him say, and, turning slightly, I saw that he was holding an orange in his hand.

'What?' Part of me thought it was funny and another part of me was nervous.

Ian's teeth were white in the moonlight. 'Come on, Jennifer,' he tried to persuade me, and the next moment he had put the orange under his chin and was moving towards me.

I had to laugh then; he looked so funny. But it was a nervous kind of laugh and as he got closer and closer to me, my laughter slowly disappeared. It was still a ridiculous situation; he was still trying to pass the orange to me from under his chin but while he was trying to pass the orange, he was looking deep into my eyes and his mouth was really close to mine. It was just as if he was moving close in order to kiss me . . .

'Jennifer . . .' he breathed, and suddenly he *was* kissing me, and neither of us noticed when the orange fell onto the sand.

The kiss went on for ages and ages. My body began to feel weak. If he hadn't eventually pulled back a little to speak, who knows what might have happened. But he did.

'Jennifer,' he said to me softly, 'you know this is right, don't you? You and me.'

And I could only stare up at him in complete shock. Because of all the things he could have said, Ian had somehow managed to use the exact same words Gary had used to me at his flat after our dinner date.

'Jennifer,' he'd said, 'you know this is right, don't you? You and me. I can give you so much pleasure. Don't feel guilty about it. Stay with me.' And I had. And afterwards he tried to blackmail me and now I've broken Pete's heart.

'No,' I said to Ian, shaking my head. 'It *isn't* right. It's wrong, very wrong.' And as I pushed him away from me and ran quickly up the beach towards my hut, I felt quite proud of myself. If Ian really likes me, then he'll understand. I have to sort things out with Pete first. Maybe then I'll feel more sure of what I want. At least, I hope I will.

Chapter 9   *Man hunting*

Lisa

Why does anyone willingly make a fool of themselves with fruit, I wonder? I really don't know, but that's what I did yesterday evening. With oranges, to be exact. Four of them. Holding them under my chin (one at a time) and desperately trying to pass them to my neighbour. At the time it seemed fun, even important to get it right. Until I realised it was almost day fifteen and I hadn't managed to kiss Ian yet. Worse than that, I didn't even know where he was.

I went looking for him as soon as the game was over and found him outside, sitting on the sand. 'Hi,' I said, sitting next to him.

'Hi,' he replied, then, to my surprise, he brought out a packet of cigarettes from his pocket.

'I didn't know you smoked,' I commented.

'I don't really,' he said. 'Or at least, not often. Do you want one?'

I shook my head. 'No thanks. It's one bad thing I don't do.'

I don't think he heard. At least he didn't say anything; he just sat there smoking and looking down the beach towards the breaking waves.

'Don't you just hate it when people give you mixed messages?' he asked me after a while. 'When they lead you to believe something and then they do the opposite?'

I had no idea what he was talking about, but I didn't want to make him even more fed up by asking questions, so I agreed. 'Oh yes,' I said. 'I hate that. I believe in being honest. I don't like playing games.'

He looked my way, smiling slightly. 'Unless it's Pass the Orange?' he joked.

Encouraged, I smiled back, continuing with what I'd been saying. 'I just try to have fun,' I said. 'To live for the moment. Especially on holiday.'

'That sounds like a very good idea,' he said after a while, his smile disappearing. 'It's a pity everyone doesn't agree with you.'

By now I was so curious to know what had happened to put him in this mood that I decided I'd just got to ask him. I was about to do so when I heard the door to the big hut open behind us. When I looked over, I saw everyone was running out onto the beach, laughing.

'You people are just plain crazy!' came Mary's voice after them.

'What's happening?' Ian asked one of the crowd running towards us.

'We're going for a midnight swim!' someone told him, and suddenly everyone was tearing their clothes off and throwing them down onto the sand. Soon there were shorts, T-shirts and underwear all over the place. It looked as if there'd been an explosion in a clothing factory.

Ian was laughing. 'A midnight swim,' he said. 'Great idea!' And suddenly I felt him reaching for my hand. 'Come on, Lisa,' he said. 'This is your chance to live for the moment!'

I felt excitement rush right through my body. 'Yes!' I

cried, getting to my feet, and next moment we were tearing our clothes off too and running down the beach towards the sea to join the others.

'Don't blame me if you all drown!' Mary shouted, but I wasn't really listening. The water was warm, and we were like a lot of kids jumping and swimming through the waves.

At first the whole group of us was together, but soon most of the couples had become whispering shapes in the darkness. Ian and I were the only ones who weren't part of a couple, which meant we were soon left alone together.

'Isn't this just perfect?' I said to him softly, swimming as close to him as I dared.

He smiled at me, his teeth bright in the half-light, and it seemed as if his bad mood had completely disappeared.

'Yes,' he agreed. 'Perfect.'

I thought *he* was perfect. Well, what I could see of him. He has such broad shoulders and strong arms. Mmm . . .

'Come on,' I said. 'I'll race you to that jetty over there!'

'All right,' he agreed, and swam off straightaway.

'Hey!' I cried. 'I wasn't ready!'

He won, of course, but then I intended him to. By the time I joined him at the jetty he was smiling broadly, and when we looked back towards the shore, we saw that there was hardly anyone left in the water. One by one the couples were making their way to bed.

'Looks as if it's just us now,' I said, doing my best to keep my voice casual.

Ian looked at me. I couldn't tell what he was thinking.

'Fancy another race?' I asked, and he smiled.

'What for? I'd only beat you again.'

'Not necessarily,' I said, wondering why he didn't kiss me. We were as close together as it was possible for two people to be without actually touching, and there was nobody else around. Not only that, but the moon was out. What was stopping him? Surely he wasn't going to be faithful to that boring Caroline?

Suddenly I couldn't wait any longer. 'What's that?' I asked, pointing at a rock and making my voice sound terrified. 'It looks like a shark!'

'Where?' Ian looked into the darkness, and while he did so, I took the opportunity to throw myself into his arms.

'Oh, Ian,' I cried. 'I'm frightened!'

Automatically his arms tightened around me. 'It's only a rock,' he said, looking down at me.

'Oh,' I breathed, staring up into his eyes innocently, 'is it?'

He looked down at me for a while, shaking his head. I could tell he hadn't been taken in by my frightened act. 'Lisa,' he said, 'you are evil.'

But he kissed me anyway. Well, of course he did, and the kiss was just amazing. I honestly can't remember when I last felt so much for someone. Even Sven didn't drive me so crazy that time in Mexico.

Then Ian pulled back. 'Lisa,' he said, 'you're lovely, absolutely lovely . . .'

'So are you, Ian,' I breathed, trying to drag his body back to mine. 'So are you.'

He pulled away again. 'But I can't do this. Not until I've broken things off with Caroline. It just wouldn't be fair.'

'Oh,' I said, feeling bitterly disappointed. *And* a little annoyed, if I'm honest. After all, what do I care about

Caroline? If the stupid woman ends up losing her boyfriend because she's so boring, then that's hardly my fault.

Still, at least I know now that Ian feels the same way about me as I feel about him. All I need to do is to make sure he breaks up with Caroline as soon as possible.

'They've got a phone here,' I told him. 'You could ring her.'

He paused, then smiled at me. 'OK,' he said. 'I will. First thing tomorrow.'

'Why not now?' I frowned.

'Lisa,' he said, 'it's one o'clock in the morning and the office is closed. *And* I'm not even sure where Caroline is. She had to stop over at Houston on the way back. I could probably find out the name of her hotel, but not at this time in the morning. I'll phone tomorrow, OK?'

'OK,' I said unwillingly, following him as he started to swim back towards the shore.

* * *

Of course, his phone call to Caroline was the very first thing I thought about when I woke up this morning. But I didn't manage to ask him about it until after breakfast, because we had to pack our bags ready to head on to Belize City.

When I did catch up with him, the news wasn't good. 'I haven't been able to speak to Caroline yet,' he said. 'The phone was out of order. I'll have to try later from Belize City.'

I was disappointed, and I'm sure it showed.

'Don't worry,' he said. 'Everything will be all right. By the way, that's a nice top you're wearing.'

I cheered up. 'Oh,' I said, sticking my chest out, 'do you think so?' It was low-cut, sexy and black and I'd chosen it especially.

'Come on, you guys,' Mary said, coming up behind us. 'Time to get on the bus.'

The plan today, before returning to Belize City, was to go to a place called Lamanai to look at yet more Mayan ruins. Getting there involved travelling by boat along a jungle river for an hour and a half, and I was determined Ian and I would be in a boat together. That way he could look at my low-cut top as much as he wanted to. And perhaps I could persuade him that a private walk in the forest would be much more interesting than looking at yet another lot of boring old ruins.

But it didn't work out like that. I made sure I sat next to Ian on the bus, and I stuck to him at the boat station while we were waiting to board our boat. Then, just at the wrong moment, Mary decided to talk to me.

'Now, Lisa,' she said, 'don't you go upsetting the guide on *this* trip, OK? You listen to what he has to tell you. And please try to keep your smart comments to a minimum.'

I swear I only looked away for *one second* to answer her, but while I did, Jennifer climbed into the boat to take the seat next to Ian. *My* seat.

And there wasn't a thing I could do about it. How unlucky can a girl be?

Chapter 10 *Apologies and invitations*

Jennifer

The first thing I thought about when I woke up this morning was that kiss. Lisa was moving about the hut getting dressed, but I just lay there in bed, running the whole beach/Pass the Orange/kiss thing in my head like a film. Why did I react like that? I felt such a fool. Running away in a panic as if I was a girl of thirteen instead of a woman of nearly thirty! I was sure Ian must think I was crazy, and maybe I am.

'Aren't you coming to Lamanai?' Lisa asked me, standing at the hut door with her bag.

I sat up in bed. 'Oh, er . . . yes,' I said.

'Well, you'd better hurry up then,' she said. 'See you at breakfast.' And off she went.

But in the end I was too late for breakfast, and by the time I'd got dressed and packed my bag, everyone else was in the bus waiting for me. The only spare seat was at the front, next to Mary. I didn't manage to talk to Ian until we stopped at the side of the river to board the boats to Lamanai.

He was already sitting in a boat waiting, and when he smiled at me, I climbed in next to him. I swear I didn't plan it that way; it just happened. And somehow I found myself apologising to him. I didn't plan that either. As I said, I do sometimes let things *just happen.*

'I'm sorry about last night, Ian,' I said as the boatman started our boat up and we set off up the river. 'I overreacted. I feel stupid.'

'That's all right, Jennifer,' he said. 'I was rushing you I expect. It's your own fault; you're too attractive.'

I looked away, suddenly feeling nervous. Grand ideas about the sense of spending some time on my own between relationships are all very well, but even though I'd tried, it was impossible not to remember how good it had felt to be held in his arms last night. I wouldn't be human if the idea of a repeat performance wasn't attractive to me. And I *am* human. Human and weak.

'Actually,' I told him, 'there's a reason why I behaved the way I did.'

'Is there?' he asked.

I nodded. 'Yes, and I'd like to explain. But not now.' I nodded my head towards our boatman's back. 'Later on.' I didn't want the story of my mistake with Gary to be talked about by all the boatmen on this stretch of river.

Another boat was coming up behind ours and Mary and Lisa were in it. Mary gave us a wave, and I waved back. Lisa didn't wave. She looked angry about something. Then I must have smiled as I realised what it was; she was furious because I was in a boat with Ian.

'What's funny?' Ian asked me, but I shook my head because it wasn't really funny. I felt quite sorry for Lisa really.

'Nothing much. Just Lisa's expression. I don't think she's enjoying this holiday very much.'

Ian raised his eyebrows. 'In my experience, the Lisas of this world are rarely happy. They always want more than they've got.'

'I think she's a bit lonely,' I said, but Ian didn't seem very interested.

'She'll be all right,' he said, moving closer to me. 'Look, let's get away somewhere alone together when we get to Belize City tonight. We could go out for a meal or something.'

'No!' I thought. But I wanted to say yes, that was the trouble. I like Ian; I enjoy being with him. I just don't want to get into another complicated situation.

'You know,' he said, 'you don't have to do anything you don't want to do. Dinner can just mean dinner, if that's what you want.'

I smiled a little then. 'OK,' I said. 'I'd like to go out to dinner with you.'

Suddenly there was a disturbance from Mary and Lisa's boat. Lisa was standing up and Mary was shouting at her to sit down. Our boatman cut his engine and we waited for them to catch us up, as Mary pulled Lisa back down onto her seat.

'What's wrong?' Ian asked Mary when they drew close.

'Lisa's trying to give the crocodiles an early lunch. *Me*.' Mary turned to Lisa, who was looking a bit embarrassed. 'What's the matter, girl?' she asked. 'You're in a boat you know, not on a dance floor. Or had you forgotten?'

I'd never seen Mary this angry before. Annoyed, yes; furiously angry, no.

'I'm sorry, Mary,' Lisa was saying. 'I didn't think.'

'That's just your trouble, Lisa girl,' Mary stormed on. 'You *never* think! Boats are for sitting still in, not for making sudden movements that almost knock people into the water!'

'Sorry,' we heard Lisa say again. 'It's just that I suddenly remembered the message you told me to give to Jennifer yesterday.' Lisa looked in our direction, calling out to me. 'Jennifer,' she shouted loud enough for everyone in the group to hear, 'your fiancé phoned yesterday. He said to tell you it's all right. It isn't too late. He wants you to phone him.'

'I've told her that already,' Mary said impatiently, but I hardly heard her. I was too busy feeling guilty again. Because somehow, what with lying awake half the night remembering how it had felt to be in Ian's arms, I'd forgotten all about trying to phone Pete again.

Over in the other boat, Mary seemed to be doing her best to control her anger. 'Come on,' she said to the boatmen. 'I guess we'd better get going. The others will be wondering where we are.'

I could feel Ian's eyes on me, but I deliberately avoided looking in his direction. Instead, I turned my head towards the passing river banks, pretending to look for crocodiles. I didn't want to discuss the whole Pete thing with Ian just then. It was all such a mess, and I hoped that by the time we went out for dinner later, I would have had a chance to speak to Pete.

When we reached Lamanai, we were given a tour around the ruins and told more stories about Mayan culture. Then we were taken on a guided walk along some of the forest paths surrounding the area.

I felt happier in the forest. It was slightly cooler in the shade of the trees for a start, and the wonderful smell from the wet leaves and damp ground instantly began to work its magic on me again.

'I'd like to be able to bottle this smell and take it home with me,' I told Ian, and as he laughed, I caught sight of Lisa's expression. She was looking *furious*. I did my best to forget about her and to concentrate on what the guide was telling us about leaf-cutter ants instead. I wanted to know about them; I'm interested in nature.

'Even though they are so small, these insects are able to carry pieces of leaf that are many, many times larger than their own bodies,' he said. 'They are very determined insects. When you are walking in the forest, you might see what you think is a long green snake on the path ahead of you. But when you get closer, you'll be surprised.'

'Jennifer,' Lisa whispered loudly into my ear, her voice sounding as unfriendly as a snake and as determined as a leaf-cutter ant. 'There's something you need to know.'

The tour guide looked over in her direction. So did Mary. She was frowning.

'As you approach,' the tour guide continued, 'you will find that the long green snake is not a snake at all, but is, in fact, thousands of leaf-cutter ants, each one holding a very large piece of leaf.'

'Last night,' Lisa said, still in that loud whisper, 'while you were in bed . . . '

'This ability of the ant to hold on to something tightly in this way was very useful to the ancient Mayans.'

'Ian and I . . . ' Lisa went on.

'Shh!' Mary said crossly.

The tour guide raised his voice. 'When the ancient Mayans had a cut or a wound, they would often take a leaf-cutter ant and they would break off its head to use its strong front legs to hold the wound closed. Come. Let's find an ant and I'll demonstrate this to you.'

The guide walked on along the path, but Lisa grabbed hold of my T-shirt, a bit like a leaf-cutter ant grabbing hold of a wound.

'What *is* it, Lisa?' I asked her crossly.

She waited until everyone had moved away before she spoke. 'Ian's mine,' she told me then. 'We were together last night. You're making a fool of yourself by throwing yourself at him. You've got a fiancé anyway. Why isn't that enough for you?'

I could have told her I'm not in love with Pete; that I want more from life than he has to offer me; that I feel confused and weak and attracted by excitement. But Lisa turned and walked quickly away before I had the chance to answer her, so I didn't.

Anyway, I felt as if I'd had quite enough of Lisa and her demands. She's a pain, and if I want to have dinner with Ian, then I will. My friend Gina used to get me to do what she wanted me to do because I liked her so much. It gave her power over me, I suppose. But it's different with Lisa. She certainly *isn't* my friend, so she isn't going to stop me doing what I want to do. Definitely not!

Chapter 11   *War*

Lisa

Back home at the Black Bull, and with Mum to look after, I sometimes feel very trapped and helpless. But it's different on holiday, and I don't intend to just sit back and wait to see what happens.

The way I see it, there are two reasons why Ian and I have only kissed once. One reason is called Caroline, and the other reason is called Jennifer.

There's nothing much I can do about Caroline except wait for Ian to phone her. But I can certainly do something about Jennifer, and what's more, I have. Right after our conversation at Lamanai.

As soon as we were back on the road to Belize City, I told Mary I had to make an urgent phone call home. She wasn't very happy about it, but she asked the driver to stop anyway. And of course, I didn't phone home at all; I phoned Pete. I took out the piece of paper I'd written his number down on, and I phoned him and told him that Jennifer was really sorry about the way she'd behaved. I told him she still loved him.

'Why isn't she phoning me herself if she's so sorry?' he asked.

It was a good question. I thought quickly. 'Because she feels she's treated you so badly,' I said. 'She thinks you won't forgive her.' There was a listening silence on the other end of the line. It was strange to think that Pete was thousands of miles away in London. He didn't sound as if he was, even though the telephone I was using was inside a bar with a view of the ocean and palm trees from the window.

'Do you really think she cares about me?' he asked at last, sounding upset and hopeful at the same time.

'I *know* she does,' I said. 'Listen, we've been sharing a room for over two weeks and we've become very good friends. She definitely thinks a lot of you. Last night I don't think she got any sleep at all. She was just lying awake crying into her pillow.' I paused, wondering whether I'd overdone it.

'But if she won't phone me herself,' Pete said at last, 'I don't see what I can do. I'll just have to wait to speak to her when she comes home.'

'No!' I said urgently; a little too urgently.

'Why not?' Pete asked reasonably enough, and I had to think quickly again.

'Well because . . . ' I decided to tell him a half-truth. 'Well, to be honest, there's a man out here who's very keen on her. He's the type who's determined to get what he wants, and he seems to want Jennifer. And what with her feeling so upset about you, she's bound to turn to someone who seems to want to comfort her . . . '

By now Pete was sounding really upset. 'I don't believe it!' he said in a voice which suggested that he did actually believe it only too well. 'This is turning into a nightmare. What do you think I should do?'

'Why don't you try to get a flight over here?' I suggested. 'Get a flight to Belize City. We'll be there by tonight, and then, you can tell Jennifer how you really feel. I expect you could even get married out here! This is a perfect place for a honeymoon!'

I did feel a little guilty as I returned to the bus, because Pete sounds like a really nice guy. But my guilty feelings only lasted until I climbed back on board the bus . . . and saw Jennifer and Ian sitting close together at the back, laughing about something. Jennifer was staring into Ian's eyes like a lovesick teenager. Either she didn't believe what I'd said about Ian and me, or she didn't care. Well, we'll see how she feels when Pete turns up with a wedding ring and a priest!

Unfortunately it's going to be quite a while before Pete can get to Belize City. I told myself I'd just have to shadow Jennifer wherever she went, to make sure she and Ian were never alone together.

But luck still wasn't on my side. When we arrived at our hotel in Belize City, it was to discover that, for the first time in the entire holiday, Jennifer and I had been given separate rooms.

'You don't look very pleased about it, girl,' Mary said. 'The hotel has an empty room, so I thought you and Jennifer would enjoy a little space.'

How right Mary would have been only a few hours before! But now everything had changed. 'Yes. Thanks, Mary,' I said, doing my best to smile, but unable to keep my voice from sounding flat and disappointed. It would have been so much easier to keep an eye on Jennifer and Ian if we'd still been sharing a room. Now I wouldn't know what was going on. And sure enough, by the time I'd unpacked my things, had a shower and made my way back down to reception, the keys to both Jennifer and Ian's rooms were hanging up on their hooks behind the reception desk. It didn't take a superior amount of intelligence to guess they were together.

Feeling totally depressed, I made my way to the hotel bar, sat there with my back to the view of the sunset and ordered a long glass of rum. There was little point in trying to find them; Belize City is a big place.

Mary joined me at the bar. I'd been so full of my miserable thoughts, I hadn't noticed her come in. Taking one look at my face, she shook her head. 'You all on your own?' she asked, and I nodded.

'Yes. You don't know where Ian and Jennifer have gone, do you?'

She shook her head. 'Sorry, no idea.' She kept on looking at me and sighed. 'Lisa, Lisa,' she said. 'If you tried to enjoy this beautiful country of mine a little more and stopped your complaining, then maybe people would want to be with you. But you just don't seem to be interested.'

By this time I felt too fed up to pretend so I said nothing, just shook my glass to make the pieces of ice knock together.

Mary sighed. 'You know,' she said, 'you make me cross sometimes, but somehow I do still like you.'

I looked up at that. 'Do you?'

She pulled a face and shook her head some more. Then she smiled at me. 'Yes,' she said, 'I do. Look, my Aunt Rose lives in Belize City. I'm going to visit her tonight for dinner. She'll be happy for you to come too if you'd like. You could see what a real home in Belize is like.'

I did my very best to smile, because I know Mary was

trying to be nice to me by offering this invitation. But the truth was, I didn't feel like moving from the bar until I'd had a whole lot more rums. On the other hand, I knew I'd only get bored with my own company, and Aunt Rose's might be better than nothing, even if it didn't sound like a very exciting evening.

'All right,' I said. 'I'll come.'

Mary gave a satisfied nod. 'Good.'

We left soon afterwards, turning off Southern Foreshore and leaving the water behind us, as we headed up towards the Court House.

We've been in Belize City before on this holiday – right at the beginning of the tour – and as Mary and I walked along now, my thoughts returned to that time. It was right at the beginning of my holiday and I was still feeling excited and keen to find out all about a new country: the busy, colourful streets of wooden buildings; the fruit on sale in the market; signs advertising boat trips to exciting-sounding places; I loved it all. That was *before* I realised that Jennifer and I were the only single people in the group, and that we'd be in competition with each other.

'Aunt Rose lives on the other side of the Swing Bridge,' Mary told me, leading the way. 'It isn't too far.'

'Right,' I replied, trying to sound enthusiastic, and suspecting that I might have overdone it when Mary gave me one of her looks. Fortunately, however, she must have decided not to say anything, and we carried on walking in silence.

It always seems to be busy in Belize City, even at night. Now there were lots of people crossing the river via the Swing Bridge, walking in both directions. It was Friday night, and they were dressed up and looking forward to some fun. Several people called out to Mary, including some men. She called back to them all, but she only seemed equally as friendly towards the men as she was to the women, and I looked at her, suddenly curious.

'Mary,' I asked, 'have you got a boyfriend?'

She looked at me as if I was crazy. 'No, girl, I have not,' she told me, frowning. 'What would I want one of them for? Get yourself a man in this country and you end up married before you know it.' She shook her head to stress her point. 'Five children later and you've got a body like a watermelon by the time you've reached thirty. No, thank you. This woman is heading for better things than that. Another three or four years to save up some money and then I'm leaving for America. *I've* got an education to get!'

Mary sounded so certain. She was so confident and sure about what she wanted in life, and I felt really jealous of that confidence. But then I expect it's easy to be so certain when you're free, without any responsibilities. And in a way, *I'm* certain about my plans and dreams too. I want to move to London, have my own flat and a good job with lots of money. And I want an exciting boyfriend. Someone who knows London and enjoys going out. But you can't always have what you want, can you?

By the time we arrived at Rose's house a few minutes later, I was feeling more miserable than ever. But Rose and her house were the opposite of miserable. The house was painted bright pink with a blue door and blue windows. Inside was just as bright, and it didn't take me very long to realise that the cheerful colours were matched by Rose's bright, cheerful personality. She welcomed me every bit as enthusiastically as she welcomed her niece, and somehow, within a few minutes of us arriving, all three of us were in the kitchen, preparing a meal with lively music playing on Rose's stereo.

'One step forwards, one step backwards!' Rose sang along with the music, her big body moving with pleasing rhythm as she chopped vegetables. Suddenly, to my great surprise, I realised I was having fun. I don't usually enjoy cooking outside work, but this was different somehow. Well, let's face it, everything here was as different to my life in Lower Tiveshell as it was possible for anything to be.

Rose was obviously a very happy woman, and I couldn't see any evidence of a man in her life either. At least, there was nothing lying around the house that looked as if it might belong to a man. In any case, Rose had only put three plates to warm in the oven, so it didn't look as if anyone else was going to join us for dinner. Perhaps Rose was like Mary, happy to be alone.

But almost as soon as I had this thought, Aunt Rose proved me wrong.

'When you going to find yourself a good man, Mary?' she asked her niece, and Mary rolled her eyes towards the ceiling.

'Don't go on at me again, Auntie,' she begged. 'You know I'm more interested in getting an education than in getting a man.'

'You need *somebody* to go on at you,' her aunt told her, shaking her head. 'I never heard of an education keeping anybody warm on a winter's night. Do you know, Lisa, I can't remember the last time this girl brought a boyfriend here to meet me, and that's all wrong, isn't it? If you don't enjoy a man when you're young, when *are* you going to enjoy one? A woman's life just isn't finished off without a man in it.'

Mary sighed, shaking her head. 'Auntie,' she said, 'you've told me all of this a hundred times.'

'And I'll tell you a few hundred times more – right up until you see sense!' Aunt Rose said loudly, turning in my direction. 'I bet Lisa here's got herself a boyfriend,' she said, but she soon saw from my expression that this wasn't the case and shook her head some more.

'Not you too?' she said. 'What is *wrong* with you girls today?' She sighed. 'I don't know. Me, I was married for the first time when I was sixteen. Not that I'm saying to you that you should just accept any man who shows any interest in you. No. You girls still need to be choosy; find yourselves a *good* man. I've always been choosy, but I've still been married three times. You know, Lisa, all of those men died on me.' Aunt Rose shook her head and laughed out loud. 'I think I was too much for them. I think I wore those men out!'

Mary was laughing now too. 'You see what my family is like, Lisa?' she said.

Aunt Rose laughed again. 'Hey, child,' she said, 'you know you wouldn't change any of us even if you could!' And as the next song started to play on the stereo, she began to sing and dance once again.

Helping to prepare the meal in the cheerful kitchen, I couldn't help thinking about Mum. My brother and I were fairly young children when Dad died but, to my knowledge, there hasn't been another man in Mum's life since. And it would have been so much better for me if there had; if there had been someone else to worry about Mum and take care of her. And of course, it would have been a lot better for Mum too.

As it is, Mum's life is very dull; I know it is. She can't walk far, and I'm at the pub quite a lot. Oh, she's got some friends who occasionally push her out in her wheelchair, but not very often.

Some people put their older relatives in a nursing home of course, a place somewhere between a hospital and a hotel, but there aren't any nursing homes near Lower Tiveshell, and besides, I know Mum would hate it. She'd feel as if she were just waiting to die. And sometimes, when I think about my plans of moving to London and having an exciting life, that's what it feels as if *I'm* doing; waiting for Mum to die. And that's horrible, because I love her. There just isn't any solution that I can see, and it's only too easy to imagine myself as a grey-haired old lady like Mum, still living in Lower Tiveshell.

'You two can lay the table now.' Aunt Rose's cheerful voice broke into my sad thoughts, and as I followed Mary into the dining room with the knives and forks, I suddenly wished I hadn't agreed to go there with Mary. Oh I liked Rose, and the food smelled delicious, but I felt I ought to be searching Belize City for Jennifer and Ian, making sure nothing was happening between them. There are only a few days of this holiday left, and I agree with Aunt Rose, not Mary. A woman *does* need a man in her life. Ian likes me, I know he does. He wouldn't have kissed me like that otherwise. And if he breaks up with Caroline and we get together, then I can at least visit him in London occasionally. Mum would be all right without me for a day from time to time. I just have to make something happen between me and Ian. I *have* to.

Suddenly I realised Mary was frowning at me across the table. 'Lisa, girl,' she said worriedly, 'you've got that look on your face again. That look that tells me there's going to be a big pile of trouble before very long.'

But I just got on with my meal and didn't bother to tell Mary that she was probably right.

Chapter 12   *Dinner and dancing*

Jennifer

I tried to phone Pete when we got to Belize City, but I just got the answering machine again. I'm not a hard-hearted person, and I still didn't want to leave a message breaking off our engagement, which means that by the time I met Ian to go to dinner, I hadn't managed to sort anything out, including my real feelings about Ian. Oh, I knew I was attracted to him all right, but I didn't know if it was more than that or whether I was really just having dinner with him to annoy Lisa. On top of that, I didn't even know if Lisa was lying about her and Ian or not.

It was all swimming around inside my head and I didn't feel very relaxed at all.

'What's wrong?' Ian asked, smiling at me across the table. 'Is the thing you want to speak to me about really as terrible as all that?'

I didn't know what he was talking about at first, but then I remembered earlier on in the boat and how I'd decided to tell him about Gary.

'What?' I said, no longer feeling so enthusiastic about discussing it. Things already seemed complicated enough. 'Oh, that.'

Ian stopped smiling and began to look a little concerned. 'Is it a problem?' he asked. 'Would you rather not talk about it after all?'

'No,' I said doubtfully. ' I mean . . . yes. Well, actually there's something I want you to tell *me* first of all.'

By now he was frowning. 'Oh?' he said. 'And what's that?'

I looked down into my wine glass. 'Well,' I said carefully, 'I wanted to ask you about last night. What you did after I . . . left you on the beach.' There was silence for a while, and then I looked up, searching his face for signs of guilt.

But Ian looked perfectly relaxed. A little confused perhaps, but definitely relaxed. 'A few of us decided to go for a swim,' he said. 'It was fun. But not as much fun as if you'd been with us, of course.'

I thought about this for a while, imagining everyone swimming in the dark ocean. Now I thought about it, I remembered hearing some excited laughter as I was lying in bed trying to get to sleep. That explained it. 'Did Lisa go swimming?' I asked, doing my best to keep my voice casual and watching carefully for his reaction.

He pulled a face, thinking. 'Yes, she did,' he said, 'because I remember at one point she made a lot of fuss because she thought she'd seen a shark.' He laughed. 'Quite a drama queen, our Lisa, isn't she?'

'Yes,' I said slowly, wondering whether to stop there or whether to ask him any more questions.

Ian was watching my face. 'Look, there's obviously something wrong, Jennifer,' he said. 'I wish you'd tell me what it is.'

I sighed, deciding I had to be absolutely sure. 'It's nothing. Or at least, it's just something silly that Lisa said to me earlier on. She said . . . well, she said you were "hers". That last night the two of you . . .' I paused, searching for the right words, but Ian supplied them for me.

'Became more than casual friends?' he said, and I nodded.

'Yes,' I said, 'that's more or less what she said.' I looked at him. 'Is it true?'

He looked straight back at me. 'Only in Lisa's imagination,' he said. 'Honestly. You know what she's like. Look, I'd be lying if I said I didn't know Lisa was attracted to me, but I think I can honestly say I haven't encouraged her.'

A woman walked past our table on her way to the toilets and, just as I'd done at Fido's Bar, I noticed the way she looked at Ian. He really was a very attractive man, and he was looking particularly smart tonight, wearing white trousers with a shirt that was the same blue as his eyes. It felt good to know that he'd dressed that way especially for me, and I didn't want the evening to be spoiled because of Lisa's over-active imagination.

'Yes,' I agreed, 'I do know what Lisa's like. She's a real gossip; she talks about everything to everyone and I'm sure half of what she says isn't true. That's why I've hardly told her anything about myself. She doesn't know anything about Pete either, apart from the fact that he exists. And I certainly haven't told her about the mess I've made of my life lately. But when she said . . . well, what she said about you and her, I just thought I should check, that's all. I hope you understand. I don't like upsetting people.'

'Of course I understand. That's the kind of person you are,' he said, and reached for my hand.

The waiter brought our meals at that point, so we were quiet for a while, and when we did talk again, I was happy to move on from the subject of Lisa. I believed what Ian had told me, and that meant I was free to enjoy being with him. Well, almost free. There was still that telephone call I had to make to Pete.

'So,' he said after a while, 'are you going to tell me whatever it was you were going to tell me?'

I sighed. I was going to tell him about Gary, wasn't I? 'All right,' I said, and told him the whole ugly story.

'I'm not sure how it happened really,' I said after I'd finished. 'I mean, I'm not usually the type who's unfaithful when they're in a relationship.' Somehow it seemed important for Ian to realise that.

He was looking at me seriously across the table. 'Well, there must have been something different about Gary then,' he suggested, 'something that made you behave out of character.'

I smiled. 'He *was* very good-looking, I suppose. He works in a sports centre, you see, so he's got a very nice body. You know how the staff in those places never wear many clothes.' I pictured the sports centre and remembered the very first time I'd seen Gary. He was another man who had women looking at him admiringly all the time.

'Anyway,' I continued, 'he was very persuasive. He certainly wouldn't take no for an answer.' I thought about it for a moment. 'But actually, I think it was more than that. I think my decision to go out on a date with Gary had a lot to do with me not being sure about my relationship with Pete any longer. I mean, if I'd still been in love with

Pete, it would have been easy to turn down Gary's invitation, wouldn't it?'

Ian looked away from me, down at his wine glass. I couldn't tell what he was thinking. 'And will you go out with Gary again,' he asked casually, 'when you get back from Belize?'

'Oh no,' I said, sick at the thought. 'No, I won't! Even if he hadn't gone and told Pete a lot of lies about what happened when we went out, the evening was mostly pretty boring. I certainly wouldn't want to repeat it.'

Ian laughed. 'What made it so boring?' he asked.

I smiled at him across the table, thinking that Ian might share Gary's good looks, but that was all. In all other ways they're entirely different. 'Because,' I explained, 'Gary only really talks about one subject, *himself*, and he isn't that interesting. It's not surprising he's got a good body, because he spends all his time making sure it looks good. He exercises all the time and lives on salad. When we were on the date, he criticised *everything* I chose to eat, and he even told me I should sit up straighter in my chair, otherwise I might injure my back!'

By now Ian was laughing out loud. 'Oh dear,' he said. 'I'm sorry, I suppose I shouldn't laugh.'

'It's OK,' I smiled. 'I don't mind. It *is* funny, or at least it's funny now.'

There was something very special about the way we laughed together. I can't really describe it. Ian was looking into my eyes and I was looking into his, and somehow our laughter joined us together. Maybe the wine had something to do with it too, but somehow I stopped worrying about everything. I've been at war with myself for the past few days because there's a part of me that wants to be sensible and to have some time on my own before I start another relationship. The trouble is, there's a bigger part of me that enjoys the company of men and being the centre of an attractive man's attention. Maybe I'm more like Lisa than I want to admit but, looking at Ian over the table, I wasn't in the mood to think about that. I like Ian and Ian likes me, and it's as simple as that. I'm on holiday, after all.

So when Ian asked me if I wanted to go on somewhere else after we'd finished our meal, I agreed. As we walked out of the restaurant, music was coming from several bars and hotels – American, Latin and Caribbean music.

'What about going dancing?' he asked, and I nodded.

'Yes,' I said. 'I'd like that. I *love* dancing.'

'Me too,' Ian said, and the next moment he'd taken my hand. 'Come on. Let's go and investigate.'

He pulled me into a bar where a band was playing loud Caribbean music and we were soon in the middle of a crowd all dancing together.

'This is a much better way to keep fit than sitting up straight in your chair,' Ian shouted to me over the music, and I laughed.

'You're right!' I said. 'Somebody should tell Gary!'

It was wild and fun, and then, just when I thought I couldn't dance any more, the band started to play quieter, slower music and couples automatically moved into each other's arms.

Ian stood looking down at me, and I knew he was probably remembering how I'd pushed him away on the beach. I could hardly blame him for not making the first move.

So I looked up at him, taking a step forward as I did so, and he smiled, opening his arms to welcome me. The next moment, we were a couple among all the other couples and I had forgotten all about Gary, Pete and Lisa.

Was it only *yesterday* that I was telling myself that it wouldn't be a good idea to rush straight into another relationship?

Chapter 13 *Endings and beginnings*

Lisa

It was almost midnight by the time Mary and I left Aunt Rose's, but somehow, Mary managed to persuade me to go to a nightclub with her.

'OK,' I said to her. 'It will make a change from a Mayan ruin anyway.'

Mary gave me her look again. 'Now, Lisa,' she said, 'don't start complaining again!'

'Who, me?' I asked, as if I didn't know what she was talking about, but I have to say, I almost *did* complain when we got there. Mary called it a nightclub, but it looked more like a bar where they happened to be playing music to me. Not really that different to the Black Bull on a Saturday night, apart from the people. Then, almost as soon as we arrived, Mary saw a friend of hers on the other side of the room and told me she'd be back in a moment. Next thing I knew, I was standing alone watching a lot of stupid romantic couples dancing together. The evening was just getting better and better, I *didn't* think.

Then suddenly, as I stood frowning at the dancers, I saw them: *Jennifer and Ian*. They were dancing as close as it was possible for two people to dance without actually getting into each other's clothes, and the sight of them made me feel sick. So he had to break it off with Caroline first, did he? And as for Jennifer, how could she be so cruel and greedy? Well, they were welcome to each other!

I was just about to leave at that point, and give up any thought of getting Ian for myself, when the music came to an end. While the band leader was talking, I saw Jennifer break away from Ian and go in the direction of the toilets. Ian went over to a table and picked up his glass of beer. I was by his side before he'd managed to drink two mouthfuls.

'What are you playing at?' I asked, and he was so surprised to see me that he swallowed his beer the wrong way and started to cough.

I didn't trust myself to hit him on the back; I felt so angry with him, there was a chance I might hit him too hard. Instead I waited for his breathing to get back to normal and asked my question again.

'What are you playing at, Ian?'

Ian's face was rather red, whether as a result of his coughing fit or from embarrassment, I couldn't be certain.

'What do you mean?' he dared to ask.

'Don't play games with me,' I said. 'Last night you were practically making love in the sea to *me* and tonight you're practically making love to *Jennifer* on the dance floor. I want to know what's going on.'

'Look, Lisa,' he said. 'I can explain.'

But I didn't give him the chance. 'Don't tell me,' I said nastily. 'Jennifer was feeling faint and you were holding her to stop her from falling over.'

Ian still looked uncomfortable. 'Well,' he said, 'not exactly . . .'

'You said you were going to phone Caroline to break it

off with her,' I went on. 'I bet you haven't even been near a phone.'

'Can we talk about this outside?' Ian said. 'People are looking at us.' Before I could reply, he took my arm and led me through the crowd and out onto the street.

Behind us the music started up again. Ian's face turned first red, then green, in the flashing lights coming through the window.

'Well?' I said. 'I'm waiting for your explanation. You'd better make it a good one.'

I thought he sighed but I couldn't be completely sure, because of the level of the music. 'Look, Lisa,' he said, 'I like you, I really do. Last night was . . . magic.'

'Oh?' I said bitterly. 'And what's this tonight then, with Jennifer?'

'It's . . .' He paused, and for a moment I thought he was going to produce some lie or other, but then he sighed again. This time I heard it clearly. 'Well,' he said, 'this is magic too. The truth is, Lisa, I like both of you. You and Jennifer. You're both lovely for different reasons. When I'm with you, I want to be with you, and when I'm with Jennifer, I want to be with her. There you are; that's the truth.' And he looked at me with his big, wide, lying eyes and expected me to accept that? He was brave, I had to give him that, or stupid . . . or drunk.

'I really do like you, Lisa,' he continued, his eyes insisting on making a connection with mine.

But suddenly, I wasn't seeing Ian any longer; I was picturing Aunt Rose instead, and I was in her kitchen, listening as she gave Mary and me advice about men. 'You girls still need to be choosy,' she'd said. 'Find yourselves a *good* man.' And suddenly I knew that Aunt Rose wouldn't think that Ian was good enough. Oh, she might be fooled at first. If she met him she would probably think he was attractive and very nice, just as Jennifer and I had done. But if she got to know him better, then it would be a different story.

Because I'd just realised, Ian wasn't nice at all. He was shallow, dishonest and only interested in himself.

When I looked at Ian properly again, I saw that Jennifer was standing right behind him, and I wondered how much she had heard.

'Lisa,' Ian continued, with obviously no idea that Jennifer was anywhere near, 'when we were together last night, it was beautiful. Forcing myself to stop kissing you was one of the hardest things I've ever had to do. You must believe me. You're a very attractive woman, and I really want to make love to you.'

I almost laughed out loud at that, but then I met Jennifer's eyes and knew she was feeling just as hurt and disappointed as I was. So I spoke to her over Ian's shoulder. 'I'm going back to the hotel,' I said. 'Are you coming?'

Ian thought I was speaking to him at first. 'Well, Lisa,' he started to say, 'you know I'd love to come with you, but . . .'

'Yes,' Jennifer said behind him, 'I'm coming.' And the sudden horror and panic on Ian's face, as he realised she was there, almost made up for my disappointment. I can still see his face now as he turned to look at her. He was really pale, his eyes were huge and his mouth was open. He looked as if he'd seen a ghost. It was fantastic.

'Jennifer!' he whispered, but Jennifer was already walking round him to join me.

As we walked off into the night, we heard him shouting after us. 'Jennifer! Wait! Please! I can explain everything!'

Neither of us said anything. We certainly didn't turn round, just carried on walking quickly away until we couldn't hear Ian any longer. In fact, we didn't speak until we reached the waterfront. Then we slowed down, pausing to look out at the dark shapes of the boats tied up in the harbour.

'We've been a real pair of fools, haven't we?' Jennifer said.

I didn't answer straightaway. I knew she was right, but it wasn't easy to admit to being a fool. Anyway, I just wasn't used to having anything in common with Jennifer.

She seemed to guess my thoughts. 'Perhaps we'll be able to get on better with each other now,' she said, looking at me.

'Yes, perhaps,' I agreed, but I couldn't entirely keep the doubt from my voice, and that made her laugh.

'Come on,' she said. 'I've got a bottle of rum in my hotel room. Let's open it and forget about Ian. Or perhaps we should celebrate.'

'What have we got to celebrate?' I asked, surprised.

'Being free, independent women?' she suggested, beginning to walk towards the hotel.

I followed more slowly, not quite feeling persuaded by what she was saying. It was obvious to me that she was as disappointed about Ian as I was. I still couldn't believe it. He'd seemed so nice. Why did he have to be so greedy? What a waste. At that moment, this really did seem like the worst holiday of my life.

Jennifer got back to the hotel before me, and she was waiting for me in reception when I arrived. She was looking at me strangely, and I knew immediately that something was wrong.

'What?' I said, suddenly feeling afraid. 'What is it?'

'The receptionist's just given me a message for you,' she said. Apparently you've had a phone call,' she told me gently, 'from your brother Frank. It's something about your mum. He wants you to phone him back straightaway.'

I knew immediately that something terrible must have happened. My brother would only phone me if it was really serious. Mum must be really ill. Either that, or . . .

But I couldn't bear to think about the alternative, and as I walked towards the phone, my hands were shaking.

'Would you like me to stay with you?' Jennifer asked, and I must have nodded, because she stayed next to me while I dialled and waited to hear my brother's voice.

And then I discovered the amazing news that Mum wasn't dead at all!

'Lisa,' Frank told me, 'Mum isn't *dead*. Far from it. She's *eloped*!'

'What are you talking about, Frank?' I said. 'Did you say *eloped*?'

'Yes,' Frank said from the other end of the line, 'you heard me right. Mum's eloped; she's just run away with somebody and married him without telling anybody!'

Actually Mum's got very bad legs and it's been years since she's run anywhere but, in the circumstances, I felt this was a small detail.

'But who's she eloped *with*?' I asked Frank excitedly.

'Some man who's recently moved to the next village,

apparently,' Frank said. 'A gardener. They met when her friends took her to a garden show. They're going to live in his house together.'

'But that's fantastic!' I said, suddenly realising exactly what Frank's news meant to me. I was free! I could leave my job and move to London. I could begin to live the kind of life I've dreamt about for as long as I can remember.

'I'm not sure what I think about all of this, Lisa,' Frank was saying worriedly now. 'We don't know this man. What if he makes Mum unhappy?'

But I wasn't in any mood to listen to his concerns. 'Of course he won't!' I said happily. 'Mum's always been a good judge of character.'

There was no way I was going to let Frank spoil the moment. Suddenly I was laughing and doing a little dance right there in the hotel reception. 'Oh, this is fantastic!' I announced to Frank, Jennifer and the world. 'Really fantastic!'

Chapter 14 *Dreams come true?*

Jennifer

I always suspected Lisa was a bit of a liar, but to be honest, now I know the truth about her life, I feel quite sad for her. She told me all about it in my room over several glasses of rum. I can't imagine what it must be like to be so unhappy that you have to tell stories about yourself to people you meet. My life isn't perfect, but whose is? I've still got a lot to be happy about, and I must admit, I felt sorry that I hadn't tried harder to be friends with Lisa.

Still, we're friends now, I suppose. Well, we'll never exactly be *close* friends, because we're just too different for that. But at least we aren't enemies. After three or four rums, I even invited her to stay with me for a few days while she looks for somewhere to live in London.

It was very late when we finally went to bed, but somehow I couldn't sleep. I just lay there thinking about Ian and how wrong I'd been about him. My mind was having difficulty making sense of how quickly everything had changed. One moment I'd been dancing in Ian's arms, my face close to his, and then only a few short minutes later, I'd come back from the toilet to overhear his conversation with Lisa. And what I'd overheard had shown that Ian was entirely different to the person I'd thought he was.

First Gary, and now Ian. I must be a terrible judge of

character. Except for Pete. Pete is definitely kind and good, not a shallow liar like Ian. And yet I want to get rid of him. What's the matter with me? Lying there in my bed, I wondered if I'd just made the biggest mistake of my life by not calling him back.

I lay awake thinking and worrying for some time and then, just as I was beginning to fall asleep at last, there was a knock at the door. At first I thought it was Ian, coming to try and persuade me that I'd got it all wrong about him, but then I heard Lisa calling my name in a loud whisper.

Looking at my watch in the first light of the morning, I saw it wasn't even six o'clock.

'Jennifer!' came Lisa's urgent whisper again, and I got out of bed crossly, wondering already if it really was possible to be friends with her for long.

'What is it?' I asked, when I opened the door.

Lisa rushed in without waiting to be invited. 'Oh, Jennifer,' she said like the drama queen Ian recently described her as, 'with all the excitement, I forgot all about it.'

'About what?' I asked tiredly, crossing the room towards my bed.

'I've got a confession to make,' she said, and I turned to look at her.

'A confession?' I repeated, beginning to feel worried.

She sat down on the edge of my bed, looking guilty. 'Yes.' She nodded. 'I'm afraid I've done something terrible. It's about Pete . . . '

Lisa

This has definitely turned out to be the best day of the holiday. I still can't quite believe it. I'm free! *Free free, free!* It's fantastic! In fact, I'm so happy, I've forgotten all about Ian already. Who needs Ian anyway? I'm going to live in London!

At first I was really worried when I had to tell Jennifer about my phone call to Pete, because her face went really white, and I thought for a moment that she was going to say I couldn't stay with her in London after all. That would have been very bad news, because I know it will probably take me quite a few weeks to find a flat of my own. Because I don't just want any old flat. It's got to be perfect. And I'll need to find a job. A good job.

So I put on my best sorry expression while I told her. Well, I *was* sorry. 'Jennifer,' I said, 'if I could only turn the clock back, I would. I mean, now we're friends and everything, I wouldn't dream of doing such a thing. Especially now we know what Ian's really like . . .'

'It's all right, Lisa,' Jennifer said at last. 'I should speak to Pete anyway. It's better this way.' She smiled at me. 'You say he's flying out here? What time do you think he'll arrive?'

'I'm not sure. Not before this evening, anyway.'

'OK,' Jennifer said, 'then I suggest we do something really nice with the day; forget about it all for a while.'

And we did do something really nice with the day; we went on a boat trip and went swimming underwater, looking at all the brightly coloured plants and fish. Mind you, I was still feeling so happy about Mum that I think I'd have been happy whatever I was doing. The future stretched before me, as colourful and bright as the fish swimming around me.

Coming back to the hotel later, we met Mary on the waterfront. 'What happened to you two last night?' she asked me. 'You missed out on a lot of fun! Still, looks like you've been having fun today anyway.' She smiled at both of us. 'It's good to see you two are getting along together at last. It's just a pity it had to wait until almost the end of your holiday.'

'Better late than never!' Jennifer laughed. 'Actually, Mary, can I have a quick word with you? There's something I'd like you to organise for me if you can.' She turned to me. 'You go on, Lisa,' she said. 'I'll catch you up in a moment.'

I was a bit curious about what Jennifer wanted Mary to organise for her, but I didn't pay too much attention because I was too busy dreaming about my new life in London. When I'm not working in a top restaurant, I intend to go shopping at the most expensive department stores in town. And then, on my nights off, I'll go to the best nightclubs and mix with famous people and millionaires. It's going to be fantastic, really fantastic!

As I neared the hotel, I saw a man standing in the doorway, looking out onto the street. He was obviously waiting for someone, and I knew immediately that he was Pete. I also knew that I was in love. Because, despite his sad, worried expression, he was *wonderful*. He was really tall with black hair and he was even more handsome than Ian.

Jennifer joined me. 'Is *that* Pete?' I whispered, and she nodded.

'Yes,' she told me, moving forward towards him. 'I'll see you later on.'

But I didn't see her later on. I was an hour or so having a shower and getting changed. Then, when I went to the hotel bar in search of a beer, I found Pete sitting alone looking out of the window at the sea. I looked around but couldn't see Jennifer anywhere, so I took a deep breath to give myself confidence, and went over to Pete's table.

'Hi,' I said. 'I'm Lisa.'

Pete looked up at me with sad but incredibly beautiful green eyes. 'She's gone,' he told me.

'Jennifer?' I said. 'Where to?'

'To somewhere called Ambergris Caye,' he said.

'Oh,' I said. 'Why?'

Pete shook his head. 'I don't know; it didn't make any sense to me. She said something about ocean and moonlight. I'm not sure. After she told me she didn't want to marry me, I wasn't really listening properly.'

I always have thought there was something strange about Jennifer, and now I'm sure of it. How could she turn her back on such an attractive man?

I sat down next to him. 'Oh, Pete, I'm so sorry,' I said, deciding there and then that I would help him to get over Jennifer. Because Pete isn't only handsome; he's successful, he believes in marriage and he lives in London. He can show me all the sights, all the most exciting places to go to. Yes, Pete doesn't know it yet, but he's perfect for me in every way. What could possibly go wrong? Pete's going to be part of my new beginning.

Goodbye boring countryside, hello exciting city!

As for Jennifer, I only hope her swim in the moonlight is enjoyable, because that's all there'll be at Ambergris Caye.

Just Jennifer and the ocean and the moonlight.

Cambridge English Readers

Other titles available at Level 5:

All I Want *by Margaret Johnson*
Alex is thirty and wants just one thing in life: her boss, Brad. But however hard she tries, things keep on going wrong for her. Then Alex discovers what it is she really wants.

Dolphin Music
by Antoinette Moses
The year is 2051. CONTROL, the government of Europe, keeps everyone happy in a virtual reality. This is a world where it is too hot to go out, and where wonderful music made by dolphins gives everyone pleasure. It's a world which is changed forever when music critic Saul Grant discovers what makes the dolphins sing and sets out to free them.

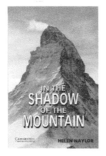

In the Shadow of the Mountain
by Helen Naylor
Clare Crowe, a journalist, travels to Switzerland to bring home the body of her grandfather, which has appeared from the bottom of a glacier 74 years after a climbing accident. Or was it an accident? Clare finds out more about her family's past than she expected and reaches decisions about her personal and professional life.

Windows of the Mind
by Frank Brennan
Each of these highly entertaining short stories centres around one of the five senses. We meet a well-known broadcaster whose blindness is her power, a war hero who hates noise and wants silence, a wine-taster who has an accident, a university lecturer who learns Tai Chi, and a magazine journalist who smells scandal and will do anything for a good story.